"Being a father has been one of the gr___t___ b___ ___ ___ ___ is to mature fully, we need a more com ___ ___ ___ ___ ___ ___ers. *Own Your Assignment* by Bethany H ___ ___ ___ ___ role and step fully into operating as s ___ ___ ___ ___ of leaders to embrace their responsibi ___ ___ ___ thy families. And active, powerful mo ___ ___ ___ ole. Their inclusion in the Body of Chri ___ ___ ___ thy, shining example of heaven on earth.

Bill Johnson, Bethel Church, Redding, CA
Author of *Raising Giant-Killers* and *The Way of Life*

"Some books share great ideas and other books are game changers; *Own Your Assignment* is the latter. I'm convinced that this book carries a precious revival seed within its pages. The book of Romans pictures the earth groaning and travailing for the sons and daughters of God to be revealed. How can sons and daughters be the transformative agent in the earth if spiritual mothers and fathers do not know and take their place?

In this book, Bethany gives language and precision to the assignment of mothering. These practical keys transcend mere tradition, and elevate the mothering identity to her proper role as world changer. I have watched Bethany both mold and model these principles. The assignment of mothering, as defined in this book is available to every woman, young and old. But here I am describing the meal when the bountiful table sits ready before you. Enjoy the feast and take your place as a world changer."

Dan McCollam, Founding director of the Prophetic Company,
Sounds of the Nations, and author of dozens of books and training manuals
including *God Vibrations*, *The Prophetic Company*, and *Bending Time*.

"It's about time someone wrote a book trumpeting the critical role of physical and spiritual mothers in the Kingdom. Our friend and colleague, Bethany Hicks, has taken on the assignment with excellence in her new book *Own Your Assignment*.

Deborah and I have been privileged to know and work with Bethany for several years and can say whole-heartedly that the message and the messenger are one. This authenticity of both person and proclamation creates a powerful expression that will challenge and inspire the reader.

In this book, Bethany not only confronts the reader with the privilege of their assignment, but lays out a pathway to transformational Mothering. It is our pleasure to recommend this book to anyone who has a desire to be part of raising up and launching a generation of world-changing sons and daughters."

David and Deborah Crone, Senior leaders of The Mission in Vacaville, CA, authors
of 8 books including *Decisions that Define Us* and *The Power of Your Life Message*.

"This is a book that I, as both a mother in the natural and a spiritual leader, am incredibly grateful for. In a season where fatherhood and sonship is often taught, the tools to equip spiritual mothers has been lacking. Own Your Assignment is filled with practical wisdom on how to steward the next generation and propel them into their destinies as powerful, healthy and relationally connected men and women of God."

Renee Evans, Co-Senior Leader, Bethel Austin, TX

"Bethany's passion for women arising and being positioned as much needed spiritual mother's in the church is fresh, challenging, encouraging and enlightening."

Tammy Hawkins, Prophetic Prayer Pastor at the Mission, Vacaville,
author of *Partnering with Heaven, Praying For Your Children*

OWN YOUR ASSIGMENT
Bethany Hicks

First Edition

Foreword by Kris Vallotton

ISBN: 978-1-09-665543-5

Imprint: Independently published

Cover photo by Amy Wenzel

Cover design by Karis Drake of Subsiststudios

Interior design & typesetting by Mario Lampic

OWN YOUR ASSIGNMENT

BETHANY HICKS

CONTENTS

FOREWORD

Mothers are the foundation of society! They create nurturing cultures that cultivate compassion, kindness, understanding, and creativity. They incubate the dreams of God and give birth to the Creator's offspring. They labor in dimensions unfathomable to men and therefore they often have perspectives of humanity that transcend intellectual assessments or statistical explanation.

Motherhood — both natural and spiritual — is not a career, an occupation, or a job. Rather, it is a heavenly call, a divine destiny, and a holy legacy.

However, the truth is that matriarchs have been absent from leadership in the Church for more than 2000 years. It's hard to imagine how profound an impact the Kingdom could have had on this planet if women would have been empowered to take their proper place alongside men in the Church of Jesus Christ. But one thing is for certain, the absence of the ones fashioned from the side chamber of man has caused us to miss out on an entire aspect of the heart of God.

Genesis 1:27 says, "God created man in His own image, in the image of God He created him; male and female He created them." Scripture is clear that it takes both the femininity of women and the masculinity of men to represent the full nature of God. Religion not only oppresses women fashioned in the image of God, but in doing so, it blinds people to the feminine side of God. This relegates them to a single dimensional relationship with their Creator and robs them of the full spectrum of the nature of the Lord.

We simply cannot continue to believe that we will fulfill the great commission with motherless families and dysfunctional fathers who are trying to carry out dualistic roles they were never designed to fulfill. While men and women are equally important, they are distinctly and profoundly different. It's past time for men to scoot over and allow our matriarchs to co-reign with us to help bring the Kingdom of God to a desperate and dying world. Simultaneously, it is high time that women rise up to understand and take hold of their unique purpose on the earth!

In the pages of this book, you will receive divine wisdom, but more than that you will be activated into your destiny as a mother on this earth. Bethany Hicks has captured the prophetic mandate that God is pouring out on the planet for this climax in world history. She clearly and powerfully releases this timely word of heaven, the understanding of the mothering heart of God, and the power for mothers to take their rightful place to rule and reign the earth with men.

In *Own Your Assignment*, Bethany has courageously taken up the kingdom commission of affirming, assisting, and accelerating the destiny of world changers, and she presents you with the opportunity to do the same. In this book, every woman who wants to change the world around them will find the clarity to apprehend this call, the courage to have a strong and feminine voice in the lives of those around them, and the divine power to take their place as a matriarch who represents the heart of God to a desperate planet!

Kris Vallotton
Leader, Bethel Church, Redding, CA
Co-Founder of Bethel School of Supernatural Ministry
Author of twelve books, including *The Supernatural Ways of Royalty, Heavy Rain and Poverty, Riches and Wealth*

.

ACKNOWLEDGEMENTS

The book of Proverbs tells us that many advisers accompany successful plans, and in the writing of this book, I couldn't agree more. I could never have accomplished this book without the love, support and lives of those who spoke into me.

To Dan McCollam, my mentor and trusted friend. The seeds for this book were first processed and strategized with you and by your help and encouragement, the message was defined, developed and delivered (see what I did there). Thank you for always seeing and valuing who I am, and continuously calling out the treasure and making room for me.

To my parents, John and Lynell Johnston, I am thankful for your love and faithfulness to the Lord, each other and your children. You have modeled the lifestyle of faithful lovers of God so well and I am forever imprinted by your example.

To my sister and fellow-champion, Heather Nunn. Thank you for your insight and edits into the content of my first draft of this book. It definitely would not be as good as it is today without you. But more importantly, thank you for being the best friend and sister I could ever have asked for.

To Regina McCollam, I am grateful for your editors' 'eagle-eye' in making the flow of this book, palatable for the readers. You are a gift to the Body of Christ and to me, and I'm constantly inspired by your heart to love and serve others.

To my church family, leaders and worship community at The Mission, in Vacaville, CA. Thank you for cheering me on as I've spread my wings to try out soaring these last few years. Each of you have personally inspired, loved, celebrated and challenged me.

To my two spiritual fathers over the last thirty years— Steve Fitzpatrick and Eric Stovesand. You both made room for a feisty young woman and were the first to truly believe in me and I am who I am today because of your great love and celebration.

To Kris Vallotton for championing the call of fathers and mothers on the earth and for first calling out this mandate and book prophetically. It was your voice that first propelled this book into reality. Thank you for being a father to many and a prophetic voice to an entire generation.

Lastly, to my devoted husband Mike and our three amazing children, Ethan, Faith and Elli. Thank you for allowing me to pursue this call and be the world-changer I am called to be. My heart is for you all to have the scope of what is possible in your lives be expanded, until every dream that's within your heart becomes a reality. Don't ever forget that you are created to be champions of your generation.

INTRODUCTION

THIS IS NOT A PARENTING book. In these pages, you will not find behavioral advice, discipline methods, or how-to's on developing your children into responsible adults; there are so many great resources already out there from qualified and trusted people on those subjects. Neither is this a book that is exclusively for natural mothers. In fact, if you've *never* had biological or adopted children or currently don't have children in the home, this book is also for you.

What this book *is* will depend on the reader. For some, it is the beginning of a conversation, and for others, it is an answer to a question. For me, this book is a mandate. It is a call from the Lord to clarify and redefine what mothering in the Kingdom really looks like in our generation. As I write these words, I can feel the internal struggle for some of being "boxed-in" by a preconceived notion of what they think a mother, particularly a spiritual mother, is supposed to look like. I completely relate to that feeling. I spent decades feeling annoyed whenever someone prophesied that I have a mother's heart or called me a spiritual mother. At the time, I didn't understand why I was reacting that way because I definitely valued that role in my own life. Now I know it was because my view of the function of a spiritual mother was distorted.

This book is a prophetic cry for women in the kingdom of God to rise up and take their place as mothers, to understand their value and the strength of their voice, and to run with their assignment to change the world around them. I believe we are all called to be world changers, but we can't change the world if we don't own our assignment.

Even now, as this powerful call to women goes out from the Father's heart, we find evidence of our world-changer purpose when God first blessed man and woman at the foundations of Creation. He said,

> *"Be fruitful and increase in number; fill the earth and subdue it. Rule over the fish in the sea and the birds in the sky and over every living creature that moves on the ground."*

> *Genesis 1:28*

We were created to change the world.

We were created to change the world. Understanding this mandate is vital for us as children of God who are carrying out the fully-realized will of the Father on the earth. We see evidence of those who don't know they were created to change the world around them. They are lost, wandering, and aimless. But they are not hopeless. They just need to wake up to the reality of their

2

identity and purpose! Whether we are aware of Who created us or not, each of us feels that sense of being made for something bigger than we even know. I believe every person on the earth has the potential for greatness within them and that the enemy of all mankind works overtime to suppress or distort this awareness in each world changer. This is where the assignment of motherhood comes in.

Though this book is primarily targeted to women, I believe that men will also benefit as they read this and catch the vision of what a powerful mother looks like and what she brings to the earth. Every man has a mother, a sister, a daughter, or a friend—and every man, woman, and child will profit from powerful women walking in God's assignment for motherhood in their lives. Who *wouldn't* want a mother speaking into and encouraging the vision of his or her life, championing and strengthening you along your path, and helping to further the tremendous and glorious call of God on you? These are all parts of the unique assignment given to mothers, both natural and spiritual. When women realize this aspect of their identity and assignment, it's going to be a game-changer in God's kingdom and throughout the earth.

> *Every man has a mother, a sister, a daughter, or a friend—and every man, woman, and child will profit from powerful women walking in God's assignment for motherhood in their lives.*

While many of the examples I use in this book come from my own personal experience as a natural mother to my children, this book is primarily to be understood in the context of the assignment of motherhood as a whole, which includes both natural and spiritual mothering. Just as Jesus used relatable parables to speak to deeper truths, I will often use stories to represent spiritual values and principles that can be applied to all women yet especially to those who are willing to take on the challenge and call of influencing and impacting those around them. This message is for every woman on earth, and every woman can step into this powerful assignment no matter her culture, ethnicity, age, or station of life.

As you will see laid out in this book, this call is not for the faint of heart, which is why I believe the Lord gave this mothering assignment particularly to women. From the very beginning, women were created to be strong, powerful, and uniquely different than men. It is brilliant how the differing genders complement and enhance one another with their strengths! Within the context of family, we see a synergistic effect of men and women functioning at an even greater level when they co-labor together. Kingdom mothers and fathers who are running together and operating within their unique assignments will release an exponential level of impact and influence on the earth.

As you read this book, my prayer is that you would awak-

> *Kingdom mothers and fathers who are running together and operating within their unique assignments will release an exponential level of impact and influence on the earth.*

en to a new sense of purpose and assignment, not just as a powerful woman but as a powerful mother in the kingdom of God. While this book is the beginning of a conversation, it is certainly not the final say on all that is encompassed within this assignment. There is much more to explore and understand within this powerful role, but for now, I pray this book will be a catalyst for your own life.

Don't discount yourself as a natural or spiritual mother like I did for years. There has been a tremendous gap in the family of God for far too long, and it's time for women to stand in that gap because we are the only ones who can. I hope you'll take this journey with me to discover God's design for motherhood because the world needs you! This is the time for women to arise and own their assignment to raise up the world changers around them.

PART I

DEFINING THE ASSIGNMENT

Chapter 1

Searching For Mothers

I GREW UP IN A STRONG, Christian family with amazing and godly parents. I am so grateful that I had such a healthy and stable upbringing, especially in a day and age when so many haven't shared this same experience. In fact, I come from a long lineage of ministers where both my paternal grandparents and my great-grandmother were ordained under the ministry of the powerful evangelist Aimee Semple McPherson. I find that fact exceptional since women in that era were only beginning to be recognized and allowed to lead in the church. To have both my grandmother and great-grandmother as trail-blazers for me, my sister, and now our daughters is such a privilege.

Yet even with this incredibly rich heritage, there were distinct seasons in my life when I was looking for a spiritual mother. I needed someone who could mentor, challenge, and encourage me. I needed someone to answer the questions I had on my heart that only a spiritual mother could speak to. Though I had strong, godly parents and two amazing spiritual fathers who embraced me and made room for me to grow in ways that marked and changed me forever, my heart was still yearning for a spiritual mother. I looked high and low and even approached a couple of women, but ultimately, I did not receive the kind of connection my heart and spirit was looking for. It certainly wasn't anyone's fault that my expectations were not met. Perhaps it was because I didn't understand what the function of a spiritual mother should be and, therefore, did not know how to identify what I was even searching for. I think there just wasn't language for this idea back then, and honestly, even in my many conversations with men and women today, there is still only a vague and abstract idea of what mothering looks like in the Kingdom.

This scarcity of mothering in the Kingdom speaks less to availability and more to misunderstanding of the assignment. You cannot step into what you do not understand. You cannot own what you do not know you are carrying. I believe the time is ripe for women to own who they are and be the mothers they are called to be. For this reality to manifest, a greater understanding of the function, role, and assignment a mother carries and how it is distinctly different than what a father carries is required. If fathers could do it all, we wouldn't need mothers, and vice versa! Because men and women were each created uniquely by God with differing abilities and capacities, fathers and mothers also carry distinct roles and functions within their parenting spheres. Knowing and valuing what you carry and what you do *not* carry is key to the

synergy of raising world changers together as spiritual parents.
It is time for women to advance
into their God-given authority
to raise up the next generation
of world changers as mothers.
We were made for this, and the
family of God will never be fully complete until mothers arise.

> *Knowing and valuing*
> *what you carry and what*
> *you do* not *carry is key*
> *to the synergy of raising*
> *world changers together as*
> *spiritual parents.*

Revealing God As Father

I have served as a worship leader for many years, and
one of the things I've observed is that when God is revealing a particular aspect of His nature to the body of Christ,
it is often reflected in the songs we sing. Because worship
is essentially meditation, when you sing the same words
over and over with a catchy melody, their message gets into
your spirit and has the power to unravel lies and establish
truths about God and yourself, sometimes without you
even knowing it. For example, in the last decade or so, one
of the powerful attributes God was revealing about Himself was that He is a good Father. In 2016, the worship song
Good Good Father won the Gospel Music Association Dove
Award in the United States for Song of the Year. This song
released a vital revelation that is foundational in our faith—
knowing that God is a good Father, and His love and goodness towards us will never change no matter what we do.
That same year, another powerful song was released about

11

our identity as children of God. The song *No Longer Slaves* took the Worship Song of the Year award. These powerful songs were not recognized because of their catchy melodies alone. They were striking a chord in the heart of the Church around the globe and shifting the mindset of a generation with the truth that He was currently revealing—the truth that He is indeed a good Father and we, in fact, are His dearly beloved children. The awards given were just small signs of the greater impact these messages had on people's lives in transforming their identities as His sons and daughters.

The revelation that God is our Father works in tandem with the reality that we are His children. They always go together. You can't truly know who you are without first knowing Him because we are created from His imagination, His heart. God is always our starting and ending point, our True North. You will never know who you truly are outside of who He is and who He says you are. Dan McCollam says, "*The truest thing about you in the universe is who heaven says you are.*"

> *God is always our starting and ending point, our True North.*

We have seen such a life-altering shift as men and women around the world are finally realizing who their Father is, that He is good, and that He does, in fact, love them deeply. Because of this revived revelation of God being a good Father, we are now seeing men in the Kingdom progressively understand more of what their role and function is as good fathers. They are seeing themselves in this big picture of Kingdom family, and it's transforming our generation!

In the midst of this great unfolding of fatherhood in the Kingdom, I've observed many women who have sat on the sidelines cheering on the men who have been discovering their voices as spiritual fathers. Unfortunately, many women have not realized that in the process, they've pulled themselves out of their own game causing the question to arise in the hearts of families everywhere, *where are the mothers?* Women, we were not created to be benchwarmers. Now is time to get off the bench, join the team, and make our voices heard!

Where are the Mothers in the Kingdom?

This is not to say that there are no mothers — particularly spiritual mothers — in the Kingdom, but they seem to be few and far between. I believe it's because motherhood has yet to be clearly defined. According to the ancient prophet Habakkuk, unless the vision becomes clear, the runner cannot carry out the message with understanding.[1] I believe this truth applies to women particularly in this context of spiritual mothering. The vision of Kingdom motherhood has yet to be made clear, and as a result, women have not owned the assignment and are, therefore, not operating in the call. In the upcoming chapters, my desire is to make the vision plain so that the women of the earth can run fast and focused in their world-changer assignment.

---

1   Habakkuk 2:3

Chapter 2

Shattering
the Motherhood Mold

T HE FIRST TIME I WAS CALLED a mother caught me off guard. Our firstborn, Ethan, was only two weeks old, and I was on a quick solo trip to the local grocery store to pick up a few needed supplies. I ran into a couple of friends from church who, within the context of our dialogue, closed our conversation with, "See you later, mama!" I immediately jolted and almost corrected them. Of course, I loved my newborn son and was stepping comfortably into my new role as his mother. I was startled because up until that point in my life, I had been known as a woman, friend, co-worker, and wife; now suddenly, I was struck by my new *identity* as a mother. Honestly, it was a shock to my system, and at the time, I wasn't prepared for the full weight of it. I realize this may seem contrary to how many women experience becoming a mother for the first time as well as to those who are yet longing for that first-time experience. But for me, it was challenging to step into this

14

brand new identity because of the definition I had associated with the term "mother."

Now, 17 years later, I have fully loved and embraced being affectionately called Mom by my three amazing children. Every day is an adventure with these unique people God has given to my husband and me, and I wouldn't trade it for anything. However, my journey of understanding what motherhood is, not only in the natural but in the spiritual, has led me on a path I did not expect.

My Own Calling As a Spiritual Mother

Over the last two decades, I have received many powerful prophetic words that have all spoken into my heavenly identity and have encouraged and affirmed my gifts and calling. Prophetic identity words such as *pioneer, forerunner, trailblazer, warrior, torch-bearer, fearless,* and *a woman of royalty* were all confirming of who I was and my activity in building the kingdom of God. I loved these types of heavenly identity words because they felt empowering and helped me feel seen and known by God in a deep and meaningful way. Occasionally, I would also receive prophetic words that I was a *spiritual mother, a lioness with a mother's heart,* and that I would be *known as a spiritual mother.* When I heard those words, I cringed inside and felt resistance to accepting them. It was not because those words weren't true or even that I didn't value motherhood. I loved mothering my natural children! These prophetic words on spiritual mothering were speaking to an assignment that, to me, seemed inferior and certainly not exciting. I perceived these words as communicating that I had reached a season where I no longer got to "do the stuff" but had to sit on the sidelines and watch others have all the fun. In my mind, the epitome of a spiritual mother was dull and carried little importance and minimum impact. As you can see, I have quite the imagination. Not only did I not *want* to identify with that picture, it didn't even resonate with who I was as an individual. I don't see myself as weak or boring, so how could I subject myself to a role that seemed to encapsulate that picture? I felt that in order for me to embrace these prophetic words of being a spiritual mother (a.k.a. power-less mother in my perception), I had to suppress and limit who I was. For years, these prophetic encounters that spoke to my identity as a mother sat like an unwatered seed in my heart until I was ready to discover what they actually meant—what the purpose of a mother really looks like in the Kingdom. And let me tell you, it may not be what you've been trained or taught to think it is. We probably all have preconceived ideas that have shaped our particular expression of what a mother looks like. One thing I now know for certain is that, biblically, mothers are powerful women who are vital in becoming and raising up the kind of world changers heaven and earth are longing to see.

What Motherhood Is Not

Before we can identify and embrace the function of what a mother *is*, it's necessary to break down the false ideas of what a mother *is not*. Many times, we don't realize what we believe until we are triggered by something. Spiritual maturity is not just about gaining new truths, but it often requires unlearning lies and replacing them with their truth counterparts.

> *Spiritual maturity is not just about gaining new truths, but it often requires unlearning lies and replacing them with their truth counterparts.*

Paul tells us in his letter to the Corinthians:

"The spiritual did not come first, but the natural, and after that the spiritual."

I Corinthians 15:46

One implied principle found in this passage would be that things in the Spirit are first seen in the natural. How we define the function of a spiritual mother is directly related to how we view a natural mother, and I believe this is where some of the misconception of motherhood as a whole has come from. Let me give you an example.

In 1966, there was a doll introduced in the United States by Topper Toys called Suzy Homemaker. This doll was very popular with little girls in that era. The Suzie Homemaker accessory line included domestic household items, functioning small appliances, a working toy oven, and even a vacuum cleaner! The doll itself was a reflection of a time where most women were still homemakers after marriage; women primarily played a domestic role with regular chores as suburban housewives. This doll and the

Suzy Homemaker name reached iconic status in America and in some ways contributed to shaping an ideal of what a mother is supposed to be in our nation.

For me, because of this subconscious Suzy-Homemaker mindset, I carried the picture that a spiritual mother was *supposed* to be passive and matronly, giving up her own dreams and metaphorically being relegated to sitting in her rocking chair, knitting little socks, and content to watch the world pass by while her husband and children were out changing it. Once she has raised those she was called to impact and they go forward with their own lives, she is left with the memories of days gone by and goes into a sort-of motherhood "retirement" looking forward to the day when she might be needed again. Now, I realize this is dramatic, nonsensical, and even humorous, but I'm telling you, many women I've spoken with personally identify with this Suzy Homemaker mindset, and I believe this attitude has contributed to the misconception of motherhood as a whole, both natural and spiritual.

The Mother Myth

In retrospect, I have no idea why this Suzy Homemaker picture was imprinted in my mind as what a natural/spiritual mother should be. My own mother does not even fit this description. And by the way, there is absolutely nothing wrong with wanting to be a mom whose primary focus is house and home. In fact, when my husband and I first had children, we made intentional choices in our lives so that I could remain at home with our children while they were young. I am so incredibly grateful we had the opportunity to do that in those early years of their lives. It is a beautiful thing for a woman who wants to and has the freedom to be a stay-at-home mom for her family. The problem with this Suzy Homemaker picture is not in its particular expression. The problem is that it's not the blueprint and assignment for all mothers. It is a misrepresentation of what motherhood is intended to look like and excludes the majority of women. The Suzy Homemaker mother is a unique expression of *some* mothers but not the assignment of *all* mothers.

Understandably, many women reading this do not personally, or even culturally, identify with the Suzy Homemaker image. But in truth, we each have our own preconceived ideas of what a mother is supposed to look like due to our particular upbringing, expectation, and cultural model. These beliefs, whether good or bad, have absolutely influenced our understanding of what mothering is, both in the natural and spiritual senses. The bottom line is, we must stop viewing motherhood as an expression only and upgrade our view to see it as an assignment.

Mother is not a personality type, and I think many, including myself, have relegated mothers to that belief for too long. The

> *Mother is not a personality type.*

temperament of a woman affects her unique expression as a mother but does not define her assignment. The assignment is an intentional responsibility that has fixed

The temperament of a woman affects her unique expression as a mother but does not define her assignment.

principles and keys (which we will get into shortly) that can be applied without exception. So whether your mother was gentle and soft-spoken or bold and boisterous, neither of those expressions define the assignment of motherhood. They were just your personal experience of your mother's personality. It is vital we understand this assignment versus expression distinction because if you believe a mother is supposed to look like a particular personality, and you're *not* that personality, you will either disqualify yourself from the assignment or confine who you are to fit a preconceived mold. Both of these responses result in a downgrade from the mission of motherhood. The responsibility is the same universally, but the individual expression varies depending on the woman.

For example, if we take a look at the medical profession, you could say that generally the *assignment* of all doctors is to administer healing. Each one of them is equipped uniquely to bring wellness to their patients, but the *expression* of their healing will look different depending on their particular area of specialty. One may heal as a cardiologist, another as a pediatrician. Still others may focus on the brain, ears, spine, eyes, lungs, and so on. The point is, the universal assignment of doctors is the same (to heal), but the expression of how they do it differs depending on their training and passion. The assignment is fixed, but the expression is fluid. Likewise, the mothering assignment is fixed regardless of age, color, race or even marital status, but how this commission expresses itself will vary depending on the unique personalities, giftings, and callings of each woman.

Don't allow yourself to conform to a false ideal of what you think a mother should look like. The world needs you to look and mother the way you do! God loves who you are, and He is excited to see what the assignment of motherhood will look like when it is uniquely expressed

> *Don't allow yourself to conform to a false ideal of what you think a mother should look like. The world needs you to look and mother the way you do!*

through you. A stay-at-home mother can raise up world changers as equally and powerfully as a CEO of a corporation. A biological mother can accelerate the vision of those who will alter the course of history as much as a single woman who has never been married can.

When women understand this assignment and are free to express it in the arena of influence God has called them to, the whole world is changed. God knows the people you are supposed to touch. He knows the sons and daughters that need your particular expression of motherhood to help them reach their fullest potential on earth. Even now, there are people all around looking for you. They are longing for mothers and fathers to see them and speak life into their situations. But we won't see them if we don't own our assignment.

Sacrifice or Suppression

One of the great universal characteristics of motherhood is sacrifice. I don't think anyone would argue that generally mothers sacrifice greatly for their families by giving of their time, energy, resources, and so much more. However, many women in their willingness to sacrifice have actually suppressed their voices in the process. I met a woman at a conference once who shared with me that years earlier she had censored her own voice as a mother so that her husband's voice could be more prominent with their children. While the notion may have seemed noble, the fruit of that choice has been detrimental for her family. She is now realizing that what seemed like self-sacrifice was really self-suppression. Thankfully, she is currently rediscovering her voice in the family, and they are all benefiting from it.

While willingness to lay down one's life is true and right, our sacrifice should never lead to our being suppressed or diminished. Sacrifice with a godly purpose is an expression of who we are and should always be for the good of those around us. When Jesus sacrificed Himself on the cross, He wasn't diminishing Who He was. He was actually revealing Who He was. His heart for mankind was shown through the greatest display of love the world has ever known. Jesus never would have

> *When Jesus sacrificed Himself on the cross, He wasn't diminishing Who He was. He was actually revealing Who He was.*

sacrificed Himself if there was no purpose to it. That would have been poor stewardship of His life. It was for the *"joy set before Him He endured the cross."*[2]

Too many women wrongly believe that for them to fulfill the assignment of motherhood, they have to silence their voice and suppress who God created them to be by insisting a father's voice be dominant. Sons and daughters *must* have the mother's voice equally in their lives. Don't call something sacrifice when it's really suppression. Don't allow yourself to conform to a false ideal of what you think a mother should look like. People need the full weight of a mother's voice, along with the father's, to become healthy powerful world changers.

> *People need the full weight of a mother's voice, along with the father's, to become healthy powerful world changers.*

Qualifications for Motherhood

Because motherhood is an assignment attached to a role given to women, this means that *any* woman can function as a mother regardless of whether she is single, married, divorced, widowed, young, or old. In fact, I'm going to say something that could sound seemingly offensive, but please hear the heart behind it. You don't need to be married to be a mother. You don't even need to have biological or adopted children to function in the assignment of motherhood. A husband makes you a wife; children, in

2   Hebrews 12:2

the broadest sense of the word, are what make you a mother. Too many women have not owned and stepped into their assignment of spiritual mothering because they are waiting for a man to validate their call. They believe a man is what authenticates them as a mother. Yes, biologically women need men for procreation, but not every woman who gives birth to a child automatically functions in the assignment of motherhood. Unfortunately, there are many natural mothers who are not present in their own children's lives due to hardships, addictions, ignorance, etc. This is all the more reason for this assignment of motherhood to be clarified and released. The world is waiting for women who will *own* being a mother.

Each parent carries something special in the family, and though both mothers and fathers functioning synergistically together is God's ideal, a mother can still be a mother if a father is not present. A father can still be a father without a mother present. Even though I did not have spiritual mothers in past seasons, I am so grateful that my spiritual fathers still spoke into my life during those critical times. Fathers are vital for family, and we will explore in a later chapter how mothers and fathers partner together in raising world changers. However, one is not dependent on the other since they serve different functions.

There are way too many women waiting for a man or a marriage before they will allow themselves to begin functioning as a mother. The assignment of motherhood can be expressed through every woman who is willing to step into it and own the name.

CHAPTER 3

OWNING THE NAME

B EFORE ANY WOMAN CAN walk out the assignment of motherhood, she needs to first personally identify with the term "mother." In essence, she needs to own the name. A natural picture of owning this powerful name of mother is when a woman has biological children or adopts children as her own. When this life-event happens, she is now essentially declaring, *"I am taking ownership of caring for these little humans. I will care and nurture them until they can do what I can do and even more on their own."* Within the context of spiritual motherhood, the principle is the same.

For women to step into the new assignment of being a mother, they need to agree with it; they need to own the name. I believe many have been negatively impacted by the lack of spiritual mothers for generations due mainly to this one point: Women

> *For women to step into the new assignment of being a mother, they need to agree with it; they need to own the name.*

have not owned the name. The ancient proverb tells us that the children of a wise woman and mother *"arise and call her blessed."*[3] There is a blessing that comes to those who own this name.

What does this positional shift look like for women? We must first agree with the fact that we are no longer *only* daughters and sisters but are *also* called to be mothers. Every woman has the opportunity to step into this assignment because it is the natural trajectory of family maturity and blessing.

As I speak into the lives of those I'm influencing spiritually and naturally, my goal is not for them to remain the same. I love and accept them where they are currently at, but I also have a vision in front of me that I am accountable to. I must do my piece in partnering with the Lord so that when my children are ready, they will be fully equipped to own the name themselves. What kind of a mother would I be if my daughters never grew into the responsibility, authority, and joy of motherhood someday (spiritual or natural) because I didn't teach them? Part of owning this name of mother is realizing that there is a day coming for our own children to possess the names of mothers and fathers and to step into their own personal journey of raising world-changers. Healthy and powerful mothers will reproduce healthy and powerful *future* mothers.

Looking back over my past twenty years, I realize that I was functioning in some capacity of the assignment of motherhood long before I owned the name. I was mentoring, leading, encouraging, and releasing many within my various spheres of influence, whether it be in worship teams, ministry schools,

---

3   Proverbs 31:28

church leadership, or even the local coffee shop I managed. Within all of these areas, there were particular people I would connect with in my heart, and I would speak into their lives. In retrospect, I think if I *knew* then who I was and the assignment that was mine to own regarding these people, I would have been more intentional in my relationship with them.

Season Shift

As women owning the name, there is an internal shift that takes place. For example, when a personal season shift is coming, two things need to take place in order for you to cross over into the new thing.

First, you must let go of the former. Second, you must agree with the new in order for the "new thing" to be activated in your life. Chuck Pierce, a prophet in our generation speaks in his book, *A Time To Advance*, "*At the end of a season, you have to shift from your current position to your destined position.*"[4] He writes that whenever God is calling us to a season shift, movement is required. We must make a positional shift in order to cross over. It doesn't work to say that you're stepping into a new season and then remain in the same place. Movement on our part is necessary to go from point A to point B.

Isaiah the prophet gives us some practical keys on how to make this necessary shift.

---

4   *A Time To Advance*, Published by: Glory of Zion International, Inc., 2011; page 141

"Forget the former things; do not dwell on the past. See, I am doing a new thing! Now it springs up; do you not perceive it?"

Isaiah 43:18-19a

One of the practical methods I've personally practiced in order to step into this positional shift of motherhood is to repeat out loud over myself, *"I am a mother. I am owning my assignment of motherhood."* This concept may seem elementary, but the reality is that many people have not crossed over into the new because they haven't made a concrete movement. They haven't said "yes" to the new yet. Your voice speaking out of the overflow of your heart's agreement is key to crossing from the old to the new.

Your voice speaking out of the overflow of your heart's agreement is key to crossing from the old to the new.

Additionally, we must consciously and intentionally break agreement with any false misconceptions of what we believed motherhood *was* so that we can embrace and own the reality of what this powerful assignment *is*. By doing this we actively step out of the old and into the new.

Knowing vs. Owning

There is a vast difference between knowing your name and owning your name. The primary distinction is that *knowing is passive* and *owning is active*. When we own our name, we are actively accepting and walking out our responsibility as defined by the name. As a mother, when I call to my children, they have a choice to respond to the sound of their name. If I call out my son's name, *"Ethan! Ethan!"* and he doesn't respond even though he can hear me clearly, he is not owning his name in that moment. Though he may *know* his name when passively hearing it called out, he *owns* his name when he actively responds to the call. When God first called to Samuel, the young boy had a choice to respond to the voice or not. When Samuel acknowledged the call by taking action, he was taking ownership of his name.[5]

Our names reveal our identity, destiny, and legacy, yet often our destiny will not be unlocked until we own who we are. When Jacob was on his deathbed,[6] he prophesied to each of his sons who they were, what they would do, and how they would be known on the earth. Jacob prophesied that Judah's line would become a tribe known for their warriors and kings. Asher would be creative with the food arts, and Dan would be judge for the people. Zebulun would live by the seashores, while Benjamin would be famous as a hunter and warrior. Their destinies and functions were attached to their names. It is the same with us.

Your seeds of destiny can be found in the name heaven calls you. As every person's name speaks to identity and calling,

> *Your seeds of destiny can be found in the name heaven calls you.*

---

5   First Samuel 3

6   Genesis 49

so the name *mother* reveals that it's more than just a term of endearment. There is an assignment of destiny and responsibility attached to it. When you discover who you are, everything you do flows from that place of identity. Like the saying goes, *"We are human beings, not human doings."* When we own the name mother along with all that comes with the name, we will flow from that place of identity into raising world changers around us.

For over twenty years I have enjoyed running as an exercise, or more accurately "slogging" (my term for slow-jogging), and I am so grateful for the discipline. It has helped me to stay in good physical and mental shape, though it has not always been fun or easy. I read an article which reported that people who identify themselves as a runner are more likely to consistently hit the pavement and run than those who identify themselves simply as someone who runs. How you see yourself matters because everything you do flows from who you believe yourself to be. A runner runs. A doctor heals. A mother raises world changers.

Everything you do flows from who you believe yourself to be.

Mindset Switch

This mindset shift of owning your name really hit home years ago when a prophet spoke to me, *"Bethany, you are not a worship leader who prophesies. You're a prophet who leads worship."* It's more than semantics or word play. As a worship leader who prophesies, I would spend my time and effort in worship looking for what the Lord was currently speaking, hoping that the prophetic word would sovereignly appear. Sometimes it did, and other times it didn't. However, as a prophetess who leads worship, I realized that *I* was anointed to release heaven's atmosphere. I was the conduit for heaven to come. My method for releasing it was secondary. I could sing any song that would release a prophetic grace, or play my guitar to shift the atmosphere, or even sing a wordless melody that would set captives free. Do you see the difference there? When I started owning my name as prophetess, everything I did now flowed from that place of authority—an authority that was present because I owned the assignment. Authority is an outcome of ownership, therefore you won't walk in confidence and authority in the places you don't own.

> *Authority is an outcome of ownership.*

When Jesus wanted His disciples to walk in a different level of relationship and authority, He activated their new assignment by naming them.

> *"**I no longer call you servants**, because a servant does not know his master's business. Instead, **I have called you friends**, for everything that I learned from my Father I have made known to you."*
>
> *John 15:15*

Jesus knew that His disciples needed to make a positional shift in their self-assessment paradigm in order for them to step into their destiny as co-heirs. They were no longer servants who were clueless as to what Jesus was up to or who only did what they were told with no questions asked. They were now to see themselves as friends who understood the will of the Father and could freely function from within that intimate place of relationship.

For the disciples to function in their new heavenly identification as friends, they needed to own the name, and we as mothers need to do the same. To live and walk out this identity is more than knowing the name or even identifying with the feelings and emotions of a mother. When we own our name, we are actively embracing the responsibilities defined by the name. The point here is not to shame those who are mothers and not fully owning the name as I'm describing it, but rather to inspire women to the reality that we need to first believe and then intentionally and purposefully own the fact that we are called to be mothers.

Living From Heavenly Identity

The Book of Judges gives us an interesting narrative about a man who was yet to own his name and thus was not yet walking in purpose. In a time of great oppression for Israel, the young Gideon was hiding out and threshing wheat in a wine press when the Angel of the Lord appeared to him out of nowhere and called him a "mighty man of valor." In that moment, Gideon had a choice to make. He had to choose to believe who heaven said he was or to continue believing the minimized version of how he saw himself.

"And the Angel of the Lord appeared to him, and said to him, 'The Lord is with you, mighty warrior!' ...Gideon replied to Him, 'but how can I save Israel? My clan is the weakest in Manasseh, and I am the least in my family.' The Lord answered, 'I will be with you, and you shall strike down all the Midianites, leaving none alive.'"

Judges 6: 12, 15-16

Here we see that God was calling Gideon something contrary to his current reality. God was relating to Gideon as a mighty warrior full of valor while Gideon, at that exact moment, was in hiding. That doesn't sound very heroic to me. Even Gideon challenged God's perception by reminding the Lord of the lowliness of his family's tribe. Gideon helpfully informs the Lord that his tribe is the least of the least and that he himself is the least of his family. Basically, he was at the "bottom of the food" chain in Israel. But that's not what God saw. God never looks at us the way we have been defined by others or by life's circumstances. In fact, heaven *always* sees us greater than we see ourselves. Much of this life's journey is discovering, believing, and walking in the truth of our heavenly identity.

> *Heaven* always *sees us greater than we see ourselves.*

Directly after Gideon's encounter with the Angel of the Lord, he received his first assignment which gave him an opportunity to step into owning his new name. He was instructed to tear down his father's altar of Baal, a false god that Israel had no business worshipping. The Scriptures record that Gideon did in fact go out and tear down his father's idols, though he did it at night because he was afraid of his father's household and the men of the city.[7] Demolishing his father's idols at night may seem cowardly, but I believe that Gideon was taking baby steps towards owning his new identity. By tearing down his father's idols, Gideon was one step closer to believing that he was indeed the mighty man of valor that heaven said he was. And as the story plays out, we see that Gideon fulfilled his assignment and delivered Israel from oppression.

We all need to know and believe what God sees in us, and sometimes we need others to remind us of who we are. Before we can *be* a mighty warrior, we must *believe* we are a mighty warrior. Before we can *be* a mother, we need to *believe* we are a mother. We need to own the assignment so we can accept the responsibility and walk it out. We need to *own* the name.

To be honest, owning the assignment of spiritual mothering in the Kingdom is still a challenge for me. Even as I write this, I find myself highly unqualified to be speaking into this topic. It's not that I'm not functioning as a mother in various spheres of influence in my life, but rather, I'm finding there are still areas of upgrade needed in my own paradigm.

Mentor or Mother

I believe many women are currently functioning within the role of motherhood but are calling it by another name

---

7   Judges 6:27–29

such as "mentoring" or "coaching." Though there's nothing wrong with these terms, I believe they both speak to parts of a greater whole when compared to all that mothering encompasses.

Women have used these terms perhaps for two reasons. First, because they are truly only operating as a mentor in someone's life, and second, perhaps because of the negative connotation associated with the term "spiritual mother." Some of these women haven't embraced the name "mother" though they are functioning as one. Because of misunderstanding the assignment or devaluing it, many women cannot identify with the name. To agree with a false definition would be contrary to the reality of how powerful they are as women. We need a heavenly mindset shift to see ourselves correctly so we can truly own the name. We must define mothering the way heaven defines it. This redefining is part of the season transition we all need to make at some point in our lives if we desire to step into the fullness of this destiny.

Walking It Out

For some of you, the issue is not that you haven't owned your assignment of motherhood. You have willingly and eagerly desired to step into the beauty of raising up world changers around you. However, you may be in a "holding pattern" waiting to be validated and recognized by others, particularly those who hold some kind of spiritual authority in your life. You don't need to be validated by man before you begin operating in who God has called you to be. Obviously, I am not speaking about dishonoring the authority in your life or those you have chosen to be accountable to, but some of you are waiting to be recognized *before* you step into your assignment. Did you know that heaven has already given you permission to begin walking in the fullness of who you are right now? There are way too many people needing the encouragement of a mother in their lives; we simply can't wait around for someone to validate us before we jump in. You don't need an official recognized position to release mothering grace to those you are called to. Time is precious. Start walking in the anointing of motherhood now, and the recognition of those who are actually assigned to you will come.

> *Start walking in the anointing of motherhood now, and the recognition of those who are actually assigned to you will come.*

Look at King David for example. He was acting and functioning like a king long before he was ever crowned or recognized as one. Samuel anointed him as king over Israel when he was a young shepherd boy, but it took over 16 years for him to be recognized as king by the people. Yet, he didn't wait that long to own his name. David immediately started functioning as a king and engaging in kingly activities. He built up an army of those who looked to him as their leader, defended Israel's borders, expanded her territory, defeated giants that threatened his people, and raised up other giant-killers at the same time. David owned the name and assignment of king long before the name owned him. He functioned as a king long before the people he was serving recognized him as their king.

> *David owned the name and assignment of king long before the name owned him.*

Just as David stepped into his assignment of being king long before he was validated and recognized, women can do the same. I believe what is needed in Kingdom families today more than anything is for women to own their assignment as mothers! Don't let your situation in life, your marital status, or your age define or limit what you can or can't do. We've got to stop getting caught up in our own misconceptions and distorted views about ourselves. There are too many spiritual orphans who need mothers to speak into their lives, and you/we are the answer. These newly realized sons and daughters need mothers who will speak into their lives with the truth of what they were really born for and show them what a Kingdom world-changer looks like. It's time for women to fully own the name so they can step into the fullness of mothering in the Kingdom.

CHAPTER 4

CREATED TO BE MIGHTY

"The harvest is plentiful but the workers are few. Ask the Lord of the harvest, therefore, to send out workers into his harvest field."

Matthew 9:37-38

J ESUS EXHORTS US AS BELIEVERS that the harvest—souls that are ready but have yet to accept Jesus into their lives—is massive and available to those with eyes to see. Even though there are more Christians being saved on the earth today than at any time before, we understand from both the Word and prophetic promises given, that there are even *more* souls to come into the Kingdom in these last days. Yet, even with the current ingathering of souls, there are countless people in the Kingdom who have yet to leave an orphan mindset behind them. They've accepted Jesus as their Lord, but they don't know how to be or walk as sons and daughters of their King. They don't understand their greatness at the deepest core of their identity, and it is evidenced by how they negatively react to circumstances, the world, relationships, and even themselves. Something as foundational as "loving others as you love yourself" can be extremely challenging when the only exposure you've had to love has been society's perverted and distorted version of love. When these orphans realize their adoption, they are not only learning who they are as beloved children of God, they are also *unlearning* lies, strongholds, and patterns that have shaped their thinking and behavior from childhood. Mighty ones need others who will see them the way God sees them and who will continue to speak the truth of heaven's identity into them until they believe it. They need the family of God. They need mothers and fathers.

Champions Of a Generation

"Blessed are those who fear the Lord, who find great delight in His commands. Their children will be mighty in the land; the generation of the upright will be blessed."

Psalm 112:1-2

It's interesting to note that the context in this passage for the mighty ones in the land is family. It is our *children* who are the champions of their generation not trained warriors or well-qualified leaders. Children are the game changers on the earth, and you cannot have children without mothers and

We are all created to be mighty, but we need family to get there.

fathers. We are all created to be mighty, but we need family to get there. Becoming the world changers we were meant to be happens in family.

As a mother, I have prayed this particular verse over my children almost every night since they were babies. I prayed that each one of them would be mighty on the earth and fulfill every purpose of God created for them in their generation. My heart's cry is that nothing would be left unfinished or undone by them. I want to see them advance the kingdom of God in their particular spheres of influence so that the world is left a far better place than the way it was before they showed up on the scene. You see, I believe my children were created to be world changers. They are champions of their generation, and when history looks back, it will see *my* children's mark on the earth.

The reality is, God created all of us to be world changers! The above verse in Psalms tells us so. It says that those who fear the Lord, their children *will* be mighty in the land. My responsibility is to be in awe of the Lord and delight in Him, and out of the overflow of that intimacy with Him, He promises my children will be powerful in their generation.

The same principle applies to spiritual parenting in the Kingdom. There are "children" out there waiting for mothers and fathers to see who they are, to believe what heaven has said over them, and to activate and equip them to become the mighty ones in their generation. Everyone benefits when champions are in the room.

Everyone benefits when champions are in the room.

"The generation of the upright will be blessed."

Psalm 112:2

An entire generation will reap the rewards of the fruit of powerful mothers and fathers. As mothers, we are fighting not only for our children's destinies to be realized and released but for an entire generation to be blessed by their impact on the earth.

> *As mothers, we are fighting not only for our children's destinies to be realized and released but for an entire generation to be blessed by their impact on the earth.*

Breaking the Lie

Though I grew up in a strong Christian home, I believed a lie from childhood that because I didn't know what my purpose was, it meant I had none. I was comparing myself to my younger sister who wanted to be a missionary from the womb, it seemed. Because she *knew* she had a destiny and my own future wasn't clear, my natural conclusion was that a purpose didn't exist for me. In fact I even believed I would die at a young age because I couldn't see beyond my immediate life. That may sound silly to have drawn that outcome, but honestly, lies don't always make sense.

When I was nineteen, my home church invited some itinerant prophets to come for a time of what we called "presbytery." Decades ago this was how the prophetic was

41

primarily flowing in my church and in many other church-es. Biblically, the term "presbytery" comes from First Tim-othy 4 where Paul was exhorting young Timothy to not ne-glect the gift that was imparted to him through prophecy by the laying on of the hands of the presbytery, or council of elders. At my church, it was a similar setting. Visiting prophets of God would pray and prophesy with the laying on of hands and impart spiritual gifts. It was always a very powerful and exciting time for our community to see how these men (who knew nothing about the people they were prophesying over) could so accurately discern and speak into the uniqueness of each person and God's glorious in-tention for their lives.

When I was chosen to receive prophetic ministry by these men of God, I remember nervously thinking as I walked up to the stage, *"What if God has nothing to say to me? What could He possibly speak about?"* Sitting before hundreds in my church community, the first words out of the prophet's mouth was, *"'You are a person of purpose and destiny!' says the Lord."* Those words came straight from heaven like an arrow into my heart, and in one single mo-ment, the Lord unravelled the lie I had believed my entire life that I was purposeless. It set me on a path marked with truth that I *was* created for something great. I was created to change the world!

These prophetic fathers spoke heaven's identity into me, and it changed the course of my life. Can our children step into their full identity and purpose without mothers and fathers in their lives? Possibly. But I believe there is an acceleration that comes when mothers and fathers are present that not only benefits sons and daughters but advances the kingdom of God as well.

Intuition and Intention

There is a prophetic principle Graham Cooke introduced into our community which we have adapted and pursued in multiple areas of life: *"When you do by intention what you've done by intuition, you achieve acceleration."* When we make the effort to understand what, why, and how we are doing something that typically comes naturally to us and then apply those values and principles more intentionally, we will experience greater and speedier advancement in that area.

For example, years ago my sister was reading a book that was speaking to her about praying for her children. Of course, she and my brother-in-law were already praying for their kids in a general way like most parents do. A particular chapter in this book triggered an understanding in her. She suddenly put the book down, got up, and went into each of her children's rooms to worship over the atmosphere, listen, and pray over each of them what she specifically heard the Father saying. When she was in her youngest son's room (who was about six years old at the time), she laid hands on his pillow and prayed intentionally for him to have dreams and encounters with the Lord. Within a week's time, my young nephew was telling his mother about all of the dreams he had been having of Jesus! When we do by intention what we've done by intuition, we achieve acceleration. Because my sister now had a greater understanding of the aim of her prayers for her children and applied that intention to what she was already naturally doing, there was an acceleration of the desired outcome.

As a spiritual mother to the worship teams I oversee, I have my singers and musicians purposely practice intentionality. We train our teams to not just *sing* the words, but to *send* the song as a message into the atmosphere. I often visualize my words going out like arrows, fashioned and created to hit specific targets as they release hope, freedom, peace, or whatever it is we are singing about. We don't randomly sing lyrics like *"There is power in the name of Jesus to break every chain"*;[8] we intentionally *send* those songs as prophetic messages to those we know need God's breakthrough in their lives. As a result of our focus, we've heard many testimonies of those who have been impacted by our intention even though they weren't aware of what we were doing.

Learning to recognize what is often called "intuition" as frequently being the voice of God and intentionally partnering with it can advance this powerful assignment called mothering. Intention will bring about an acceleration of maturity to sons and daughters on the earth, and we will witness the mighty ones arising in their own generation.

---

8   Break Every Chain, CCLI #5910977

A World-Changer Culture

Like the natural family, my church family creates a culture for the mighty to thrive. Recently, at my home church, The Mission in Vacaville, California, our senior leader, David Crone, has been re-establishing the vision of the house. Essentially, our mission is this: *To raise up and release world changers.* For many, this may seem like a lofty or arrogant goal, and for others it may sound trite or generic. In a Kingdom culture where the term "world-changer" is almost a buzzword, it can seem to lose some of the weightiness of its true meaning through constant use and little application. Yet the truth is, our vision statement is not simply a far-fetched desire for The Mission Church to someday obtain in the distant future. It is rather a clarification and acknowledgment of our *current* reality. The Mission is *already* raising up and releasing world-changers. The core leadership team of The Mission are all world-changers who are not only greatly impacting our local and regional areas through training and equipping but are also traveling around the world influencing and changing culture every time they go out. They do this whether it's feeding the homeless at the local parks or speaking to thousands of influential leaders across the continents. This mission is not just limited to a few people on the core leadership team either. There are many within the extended leadership and within our congregation who are making a significant difference on a daily basis locally, regionally, nationally, and globally. This world-changer culture exists because there is a value that has been intentionally woven into the fabric of the house DNA that we are a people who embrace the reality that we are each meant to have a greater impact on the earth, and we are going after that vision until it is manifested on earth.

"Their children will be mighty in the land…" World-changers are the mighty ones in their own generation. They are the burning ones, the bright and brilliant fire starters who are so consumed with the love and light of Christ that everywhere they go, earth begins to look a little more like heaven. This is part of the assignment for every believer; this includes you.

CHAPTER 5

LEARNING TO SOAR

T HERE IS A PRINCIPLE in nature that was originally established at the beginning of time which applies to
our subject. Let me give you some context of the principle
so the point can hit home later. We find in the first chapter
of Genesis during the account of Creation that whenever
something living was formed, it would reproduce after its
own kind.[9] Meaning like produces like. Apple trees multi-
ply into more apple trees. Elephants reproduce other elephants. Colorful Koi fish spawn more Koi fish. You get the
idea. What is sown will be reaped. Like produces like.

Imitation

Within this creational principle of reproducing after
your own kind, there is a primary key that reveals the
heart of God for mothers. The key is this: the best way
to raise a world-changer is to *be* a world-changer. Let me

---

9   Genesis 1:11, 24

explain. In the first chapter of the Book of Romans, Paul the apostle tells us that everything that can be understood about God's divine nature and eternal power can be found in His creation,[10] and as a result, we can learn patterns and principles about spiritual realities if we have eyes to see. Because we can understand spiritual truths about God and life through creation, I want to explore something with you that is found within zoology, the scientific study of the animal kingdom. There is a zoological principle relevant to our raising up world changers called *imprinting.* Imprinting happens *"when a young animal comes to recognize another animal, person, or thing as a parent or other object of habitual trust.*[11] During this learning process, a newly born or hatched animal will learn to become what they were made for by *imitating* the first "parent" it sees, one of its own species. Interestingly, when birds in particular are hatched, they actually have no clue as to what or who they are, and they instinctively look around for something to identify themselves with—something to tell them who they are. If the mother of baby ducks is not around in those early critical moments, a young duckling will easily identify with a chicken, cat, dog or even a bright red ball for the rest of its life. Now that presents a humorous picture, doesn't it? But the truth of the matter is, though the duck

---

10   Romans 1:20

11   https://www.google.com/search?ei=5UOZXK6bGYv1-gSe8YfY-Dw&q=imprinting+definition+&oq=imprinting+definition+&gs_l=p-sy-ab.3..0l2j0i67j0l7.110499.110499..110961...0.0..0.70.70.1......0....1.. gws-wiz.......0i71.SD3Au872Zd8)

would be alive, it wouldn't be living in its truest identity because it wouldn't be imitating one of its own kind. When sons and daughters open their eyes to the realities of sonship that they've just become aware of, they need someone to follow, someone to trust and show them who they are and what they are made for. They need someone to imitate what being a son or daughter of the King looks like.

Learning To Soar

This fundamental learning process of imitation is vital to our call and responsibility in raising up and releasing Kingdom sons and daughters. One of the most powerful and majestic animals in all of creation — the eagle — models this concept particularly well. A fascinating picture takes place while young eaglets are still helpless in their nest and have yet to learn to feed themselves or to fly. From birth up until they are several weeks old, the baby eaglets are regularly fed by their parents who flies out daily and brings back their food. As the mother flies out to hunt, the eaglets are intently observing all that the activity employs including taking off, perching, gliding, flapping, and landing. It is proven that baby eagles can only learn to fly by *first watching* how their parents do it.[12] If flying is not modeled by a parent or a surrogate parent, the young eagle will never learn to soar like it was meant to. It is the same for our sons and daughters. The best way to raise up

12 https://www.reference.com/pets-animals/eagles-teach-young-fly-6e492fff13d5d50

a world-changer is to be one. When we own our individual callings and purposes and know who we are in the Kingdom, our children will experience what this looks like. They will have something to pattern their own lives after. We inspire others to soar by soaring the heights ourselves. We show them it can be done and communicate the truth that if we can do it, they can do it too.

> *We inspire others to soar by soaring the heights ourselves.*

When my children were toddlers and learning how to feed themselves, they would each get to this moment where they would no longer allow me to feed them. *"My do it, Mommy. My do it,"* became their motto. They were adamant that once they were shown how to properly use the eating utensils, they could take it from there. Isn't that the point? As mothers, we model not only what is necessary but what is possible.

> *As mothers, we model not only what is necessary but what is possible.*

On November 7, 1867, a woman was born who changed the world as it was known in her day. Marie Curie was the daughter of two teachers and took after her father's interests of math and physics. As Marie grew older, her brilliant and inquisitive mind would ultimately lead her on a path to becoming the first woman ever to win a Nobel Prize. She was awarded for her discovery of radioactivity. Along with her husband, who was a French physicist, they became internationally known for their scientific efforts, and in 1911, Curie won her second Nobel Prize, this time in chemistry. She became the first person—man or woman—to ever win two Nobel Prize awards. These inspiring facts alone about this tremendous woman's life are astounding and praise-worthy, but the story doesn't end there. Marie's eldest daughter, Irene Joliot-Curie, followed her example and also won a Nobel Prize in chemistry in 1935.[13]

World-changers produce world-changers. When those whom we are assigned to impact see how *we* live powerfully within our own call, it raises the ceiling of what is possible in their own lives so they, too, can dream.

> *World-changers produce world-changers.*

Being a worship pastor for the last two decades, I have used this same principle of imitation to demonstrate to my worship leaders, singers, and musicians what is not only permissible but also possible in our worship culture. Practically, I do this by fully embracing my own sound as I lead and then by encouraging and making room for others to release who they are. When I walk in vibrant freedom in worship, it not only models for my teams their own permission to be free, but it sets a culture of freedom for our entire church community. I am not interested in duplicating myself into a bunch of "mini-me's" that are required to lead, sing, and sound just like me. As a mother to our worship

13 https://www.biography.com/people/marie-curie-9263538

community, my desire is to impart and model a value of being authentically and wholly myself which in turn gives others permission to fully embrace who they are.

In a world full of "cookie-cutters" and copycats, we actually need sons and daughters to be as God originally intended them to be—uniquely, beautifully, fearfully and wonderfully made. Unfortunately, this is not always the case. Take a look at the music industry where there are countless young and old singers striving to sound identical to the latest and greatest music artist. Just watch any episode of a singing competition like *American Idol, The Voice,* or *X-Factor.* All of these hit television shows are speaking to the reality that the world is looking for something unique, unheard-of, never-before-seen. They're looking for you to be you.

> *The world is looking for something unique, unheard-of, never-before-seen. They're looking for you to be you.*

There is a world of difference between *following* someone and *becoming* someone. Even Paul the apostle said, *"Follow me as I follow Christ,"*[14] giving precedence to following others' godly example by imitation. Children learn how to walk by watching others walk. Eaglets learn how to soar by imitating their parents. Future champions learn by following our example of changing the world, but they will have their own unique path laid out for them on what that will look like. We teach them how to fly, but they have

---

14   I Corinthians 11:1

their own direction. Don't expect them to look like you. Expect and release them to look like them.

Generational Imprinting

In the Book of Second Timothy, we see a beautiful example of this imitation principle where the apostle Paul, a spiritual father to Timothy, commends a generational faith that was passed down, or *imprinted*, through Timothy's maternal family line. Catch this powerful family inheritance in the following Scripture:

> *"I thank God...when I call to remembrance the genuine faith that is IN you, **which dwelt first** in your grandmother Lois **and** your mother Eunice, and I am persuaded is in you also."*
>
> II Timothy 1:3a,5 (NASB, emphasis added)

Lois, Timothy's grandmother, pioneered and established a new value that affected her generational legacy. She was the first one in her family to cultivate and carry a genuine faith which she modeled and imprinted to her daughter, Eunice. Many of you are first generation believers who are breaking new ground in faith for those to come. Like Lois, you are heroines who are passing the treasures of the kingdom of God to your children who then have the potential impact of shifting and transforming your generational line for eternity. This principle of imprinting then creates a domino effect that spans throughout the family

53

line. For example, Lois' story doesn't end with her daughter Eunice; we see the deposits of this faith in her grandson Timothy who eventually became a leading character in the first century church. What a powerful example of transforming and transcending your own generation. Timothy carried a faith that is directly attributed to his mother and grandmother.

What will our children and grandchildren attribute to us? What are we modeling for those we have influence over? What are we imprinting into their lives?

I don't remember a single moment of my childhood where worship didn't have influence in some way, shape, or form. Whether it was serving on our local church worship teams, hosting Bible studies, having worship music quietly playing as we noisily went about our daily chores, or watching my dad spend time in the early mornings reading his Bible and praying, my parents modeled a worship lifestyle to their children because of a value they themselves lived by. As a result, worship was *imprinted* as a primary value into all three of their children, each of whom became worship pastors and leaders of various worship schools and movements.

My parents' legacy doesn't end with the first generation after them. My sister has also modeled and passed on the primary value of worship to her three children who are now all involved with worship teams in some way. Two of them are worship leaders and musicians and the third is a phenomenal drummer and sound engineer for their worship team. World-changers reproduce after their own kind, who then reproduce after their own kind, and so on and so forth. It doesn't end, and it's not supposed to. This is how the kingdom of God advances on the earth and how we go from glory to glory.

The great evangelist of our generation, Billy Graham, brought wisdom and counsel to United States presidents, world leaders, and highly influential people throughout his career as "America's Pastor." He lived and preached the gospel in massive crusades for decades and led millions to the Lord. Billy Graham's tremendous love for the Lord fueled all that he did, yet even with the exposure to all of these world shaking influencers, not one of these infamous leaders could compare to the person who had impacted his life the most—his mother. In speaking about her, Billy is quoted as saying, *"Of all the people I have ever known, she had the greatest influence on me.*[15] How did Billy's mother surpass all of his generation's greatest leaders in impacting her son? I believe it was because she was a world-changer herself in prayer and the Word, and she imprinted to her son what it looked like to live a life fully devoted to the Lord. Billy also said of his mother after she passed away, *"The testimony of my mother's life helped mold me and taught me how to live."*[16]

Just like the eaglets that intently watch their mother and father soar in circles around them so they can learn

15 https://billygraham.org/story/7-life-lessons-billy-graham-learned-from-his-mother/

16 https://billygraham.org/story/7-life-lessons-billy-graham-learned-from-his-mother/

to fly, one of the most important keys in our assignment as mothers is to fully be who *we* were created to be so our children can be inspired and know they have permission to be their glorious selves as well. The most effective way to raise up a world-changers is to be a world-changer yourself.

> *The most effective way to raise up a world-changers is to be a world-changer yourself.*

Your High Places

The Book of Second Samuel tells us that each of us are created to have our own high places to run with God.

> *"He makes my feet like hinds' feet, and sets me on MY high places."*
>
> *Second Samuel 22:34 (NASB)*

Each of us are created for great things, and all of us are designed to soar, but so many sons and daughters have yet to walk out this truth in their lives. I believe the reason many have not reached their highest potential is because they don't actually know what is possible for them. It could be that what is possible was never modeled to them or that they haven't had mothers and fathers speaking into the vision of their lives. For example, when I was first learning how to hear God's voice and to prophesy, I thought the sum of the purpose of prophecy was to give or receive a prophetic word within the church context only. Though there is nothing gravely wrong with that, it was all I was exposed to, and it was all I knew. However, when I surrounded myself with mothers and fathers in this area who have an expanded view of prophecy, I saw what was *possible* in the prophetic. I learned that prophecy is not just for the church, but it's for all of life— business, family, education, arts, entertainment, and so much more. I discovered prophecy is a major key in releasing God's will on earth. My life and my purpose have changed dramatically because I was exposed to those who saw things *bigger* than I did and who were living at a greater level. These men and women showed me what was possible to the point that I could never again be satisfied at a lesser level of experience.

When you've tasted and seen, you can never be the same. When people "taste" by observing the possibilities modeled by mothers, they will begin to see their own purpose through a new lens.

When a generation sees what a mighty one who is doing great exploits on the earth looks like, it expands their vision and creates room for them to dream of what is possible for their own lives. Thriving replaces surviving, and they are well on the path of their own journey to changing the world. It is difficult to dream when you are merely surviving. Jesus paid too high a high price for us to just barely get by in life.

> *"I have come that they may have life, and have it to the full."*
>
> *John 10:10*

> *Thriving is now our portion, not surviving.*

Thriving is now our portion, not surviving. As sons and daughters of God, it is our promise and inheritance to thrive, to be the head and not the tail. As mothers, we absolutely must demonstrate this abundant life for a generation who is watching us to see how it is done. If our children don't see it modeled for them, they will be challenged in knowing how to walk in their own high places. It's up to us to blaze the trails of possibilities before them.

Up until now, I've been laying down the foundation to help us as women understand the vital need, call, and function of motherhood. In the upcoming chapters, we will begin to explore practical keys of the assignment of motherhood and how to walk in it as women of God.

PART II

KEYS OF THE ASSIGNMENT

CHAPTER 6

MAKING THE VISION PLAIN

E VERYTHING BEGINS WITH VI-
SION. You began with a vision. The coffeehouse, home,
or park where you are reading
this book right now all began at

> *Everything begins
> with vision.*

some point with a vision. Everything we see that was created and built by mankind was originally inside of someone as an inspired idea, a creative thought, or a vision.

Mothers have one of the greatest joys, responsibilities,
and assignments that will radically affect the future of the
earth and God's kingdom. We are entrusted with seeing and
valuing God's vision for others and raising them up to be
what He has designed from the foundations of the earth. As
we will see in the next chapter, treasuring the vision is key
for our assignment, yet before we can *treasure* the vision we
must first *value* it. You will never treasure what you don't
value, and so we begin with understanding what vision is
and why it is vital in order for destiny to be fulfilled.

Hearing His Voice

God's desire was and still is for all of mankind to be inhabited by His Spirit so that our sons and daughters could prophesy and so that dreams and visions would be an available reality on earth. In order to have or value prophetic vision, you must first believe that God has already poured out His Spirit on all flesh. He is even available to you right now, this very moment. God revealed His great commitment for this reality in the Book of Joel, and then again later in Acts, when He said,

> *"I will pour out my Spirit upon all flesh. Your sons and daughters shall prophesy, your old men shall dream dreams, your young men shall see visions."*

> *Joel 2:28 (NKJV)*

One of the things I love about the Lord is that He makes the qualifications for things so simple. It doesn't mean a believer's life is always easy to walk out, but the receiving of His gifts, like salvation and His Spirit, are always straightforward and uncomplicated. Look at the above passage where He describes the qualification for where His Spirit is to be poured out. All flesh. That's it. You don't need a doctorate degree in theology, a supernatural sign at birth, no memorization of books of the Bible is required to experience His Spirit within you. What qualifies you to receive the power of the Holy Spirit is the fact that you have human flesh. If you are reading this, it means you qualify!

If you have yet to receive the benefit of receiving His Spirit poured out on you as described in the Book of Acts,[17] I encourage you now to just ask, believe, and receive. It's honestly as simple as that, and your life will never be the same in the best possible way. He has so many good gifts to give because He is always so good.

I love this quote from Cleddie Keith, "*Nothing gives people greater dignity as sons and daughters than to hear the voice of God.*" Every son and daughter has not only the privilege but the *right* to hear their Father's voice. A mark of belonging to Him is hearing Him.

> *A mark of belonging to Him is hearing Him.*

"*My sheep listen to my voice; I know them, and they follow Me.*"

John 10:27

God is always speaking, and He has provided the ability to hear His voice to every person on the planet if they would listen. Every mother is equipped with the ability to prophesy and thus hear the vision God has for her children's lives.

Looking Ahead

Vision is about seeing, and prophetic vision is about seeing the future as God sees it. In this process of accessing prophetic

> *Vision is about seeing, and prophetic vision is about seeing the future as God sees it.*

---

17 Acts 2

vision, we must understand that God *always* wants us looking ahead and never behind us. In the Book of Isaiah, God commands us to:

> *"Forget the former things; do not dwell on the past. See, I am doing a new thing! Now it springs up; do you not perceive it?"*

> *Isaiah 43:18*

> *Prophetic vision is required to see the new thing that God is doing.*

Prophetic vision is required to see the new thing that God is doing. In the above passage, He first exhorts us to "see" that He's doing something new, and then He asks, *"Do you not perceive it?"* Can't you just hear the urgency in the Lord's voice as He is crying out, *"Who is paying attention? Who is choosing to turn their gaze to look at what's ahead?"* The Lord wants us to forget the things of the past because He knows that when we focus on the past, it tethers us to our yesterdays. We must not allow these former things to be a dead weight in our lives because they slow us down in advancing into our destinies. It's impossible to look ahead while you're looking behind. Looking back didn't work out well for Lot's wife,[18] and it is not an empowering way for us to live either.

Focusing on the past is like driving a car backwards instead of forward. In order to drive in reverse, you have

---

18   Genesis 19:26

to turn your head and look behind you. To drive forward you need to look ahead to see what's coming and to know where you are going. In life, there are times when it's necessary to use the "rear-view mirror" and look behind you, but it shouldn't be our primary posture. Looking back should only happen because Holy Spirit has revealed something that needs to be dealt with. Perhaps He wants to reveal a key to be discovered for your future or an obstacle that needs to be removed. Either way, looking back should only take a moment of your attention and always be filled with hope. I love this philosophy I learned from a powerful speaker and have adopted it for myself as a way of life. He said, *"I only give myself about fifteen seconds to feel bad about something, and then I move on."* Obviously, he is not talking about neglecting to clean up relational messes he's made or refusing to take ownership for mistakes or sinful behavior. All of those things need to be dealt with appropriately, yet once they are dealt with, be done with it! Move on. Don't pitch a tent and build a thriving community around your past mistakes, and certainly don't give the enemy any air time in your thoughts. Jesus paid too high of a price for you to be paralyzed by guilt and shame. God makes it so simple. Repent by changing your way of thinking to how He thinks, forget about the past, and keep moving forward.

As we learn to live and operate from the lens of this forward way of thinking and moving as God intended, it is important for us to keep that same lens of life not only for ourselves but also for those we are desiring to impact.

In fact, it is a *must* if we are to be effective at this mothering assignment. One of the worst things we can do is bring up past mistakes and failures *after* they've already been dealt with. Mothers are called to be vision-keepers and destiny-defenders. To hold the past mistakes of our children against them will create an unnecessary obstacle to their future. It is our joy to accelerate their future and hope, not quench it with inferior rear-view thinking.

> *Mothers are called to be vision-keepers and destiny-defenders.*

Years ago, I was involved in a relational conflict with a close friend of mine. In my process of working to reconcile with her, the enemy worked overtime to steal, kill, and destroy my identity. He certainly didn't pull any punches. During that time, I had to consciously choose to *not* believe the lies that were filling my head. Lies suggested, *"You're not a good friend," "God is disappointed with you,"* or even, *"You're not worthy to walk in your calling because of this relational issue."*

In the midst of warring to remember the truth about who God is and who He said I was, the enemy attempted to stop me from advancing a worship school that I had just pioneered in my region. He did this through accusations, fear, and self-doubt. The enemy worked hard to capture my attention with the "former things" so that I would not continue with the assignment God had given me. If I had aligned myself with the lies of the enemy or given in to the voice of shame because of the mistakes of yesterday, I never would have stepped into the new thing.

God doesn't judge or even view us by our past failures, and He certainly doesn't want us to either. Jesus did not forgive us through the cross so that we would remain immobilized by

> *God doesn't judge or even view us by our past failures, and He certainly doesn't want us to either.*

our own sin nor that we would continue to be plagued by past sins committed against us. Forget the former things, and look ahead to the new. It's not a passive, half-hearted suggestion. It's a command that keeps us on the overcoming path of the abundant life.

"Let your eyes look straight ahead; fix your gaze directly before you."

Proverbs 4:25

If you're stuck in the past, you will not advance into your destiny. It's time to catch up with Him. He's doing something new, something that's never been heard of or even conceived by human minds. He's reserved some of His best stuff just for you! A destiny that will "blow your socks off" and overwhelmingly stun you with His goodness.

For years, I received prophetic words about how what is coming will *astound me, blow my mind,* and be *better than I can imagine,* and I actually have a pretty good imagination! And you know what? It's true! Every word of it. God astounds me with His goodness, and the paths He has taken me on have absolutely blown me away and continue to do so. There are times I think I may be dreaming, even pinching myself to test the reality of the invigorating dream I am living. But it's all as real as when He first promised it years ago. You see, He's always doing a new thing, and a new thing requires a new vision—a vision that looks ahead. You were created to advance, and having prophetic vision is absolutely vital to your destiny and purpose, as it is for every person on the planet.

We cannot raise up world-changers without prophetic vision because without it, the next generation will never understand that they even have a purpose. When vision is released, people can walk the path that leads to destiny. Without vision, the path will not even be discovered.

> *"Where there is no prophetic vision the people cast off restraint."*
>
> *Proverbs 29:18 (ESV)*

This verse gives us a key to the relationship between vision and destiny. Other Bible translations read *without prophetic vision the people are let loose, show lack of restraint, run wild, etc.* This is my personal paraphrase of Proverbs 29:18: *People without prophetic vision lead purposeless lives.* Without the ability to see what's ahead, there is nothing in a person's life that compels them to intentionally move forward. Let's flip that paraphrase now with a positive spin and see what that looks like: *Prophetic vision leads to destiny.* The idea given in this passage is that vision creates a specific path for us to walk on, causing us to know our purpose. Without prophetic vision, there is no path to walk on, and we are aimless, wandering, and purposeless. Once the path is created through the releasing of vision, the receiver knows that they have a purpose and a goal. They have something to set their sights on and start adjusting their life towards, and as they do, they discover the very destiny they are created for.

In 2006, when I was pregnant with my youngest daughter, I was attending a leadership conference at Bethel Church in Redding, California. I was approached by Bethel's preschool pastor. She told me she had a prophetic word for the child I was carrying and proceeded to prophesy that this child would *"blaze a trail for others to follow"* and that *"she would have an audience."*

As a mother, I immediately started pondering this prophetic vision. I wondered what kind of gifts this child would have that would be something others would want to follow and be audience to. After she was born and as she has been growing, I have allowed these prophetic words and visions to create a path and have kept a careful eye to see what gifts and graces would begin to manifest in her life related to that word.

This daughter has become incredibly gifted in all forms of creativity. She is excellent at drawing and painting, a natural at acting, has a beautiful singing voice, and is extremely graceful in dance and movement. In fact, she is so good in so many areas, particularly related to creativity, that I am watching to see what arena she ends up choosing to focus on.

The prophetic word created a potential for destiny that has prompted me to make particular decisions that would partner with the vision, like putting her in music and ballet lessons and giving her opportunities to perform and sing in plays and youth theater. All of these things we've tried out over the years in order to give her gifts the opportunity to grow.

Samson, one of Israel's judges, was famous for his strength. He single-handedly defeated 1000 Philistines with the jawbone of a donkey, amongst other great exploits.[19] Yet the vision of Samson as the deliverer of Israel was first revealed to his parents before his conception, along with the restraints tied to the vision. The angel instructed Samson's mother to not drink any wine or eat anything unclean while she was pregnant with him. Additionally they were not to allow a razor to ever be used on his head for he would be a Nazarite, one set apart for the Lord.[20] The point is, as mothers we allow the vision to direct, shape, and create the path for what our child's future could look like, and then we give them the room to explore what's possible.

Restraints Create the Path

Once the path is clear, I have found that identifying and accessing the vision is not enough to bring it forth. The next step is agreeing with the vision. The way that happens is through restraint. Truthfully, this part is challenging for most people as we don't like restraint, particularly in the

---

19 Judges 15:14–16

20 Judges 13

context of denying ourselves something good or something we want. Proverbs 29:18 may seem to imply that the purpose of restraint in relation to vision is to hold us back *from* something. In reality, restraint in this context is there to hold us *for* something. Biblically, in this passage, restraint looks more like the banks to a river or the boundary lines to a pathway. These banks and boundary lines are meant to help guide us so that we stay on track with our purpose without getting lost or wandering off of it. Without vision there are no banks to the river or distinguishing markers for a pathway and, thus, no way of identifying where to go.

It was *"for the joy set before Him"* that Jesus endured the cross.[21] Jesus had a prophetic vision of the joy that was ahead for Him in knowing we would be brought into His kingdom, and He let nothing and no one deter Him from the path of His destiny as Savior of the world. It was this joy that created His path and Jesus' agreement with this vision that kept Him on it all the way to Calvary.

As I mentioned earlier, I have been running for almost three decades, but I don't run because I love the sheer action of it as some do. My value for running is more about the benefits it gives me in staying in moderately good shape and feeling good both physically and emotionally. Years ago, I decided to run a half-marathon, which meant I had to follow a rigid training program that outlined for me what to eat, how often I had to train and rest, the intensity of the workouts and frequency, etc. All of these

---

21   Hebrews 12:2

"boundaries" established by my training program were guaranteed to help me run my best half-marathon. I know, many of you are thinking how can *best* and *half-marathon* even be in the same sentence, and I completely understand. It was certainly challenging, but I was determined to accomplish this goal that I had set for myself, and so I submitted myself to the restraints attached to the vision. Race day was the vision, but the training process was my boundary line.

Likewise, prophetic vision determines the *what* and the *how* of partnering with the Lord to see a promise come to fulfillment. The vision determines the restraints or boundaries. If someone has a vision of becoming a doctor or a nurse, then that vision sets the course direction of what to say yes to and what to say no to so that the desired goal can be reached. When an author friend of mine wanted to write six books in one year, he did it by putting boundaries in his daily schedule so the goal could be reached, and it was! The vision determines the boundaries; the boundaries advance the vision; and the way those two realities merge is through our agreement.

> *The vision determines the boundaries; the boundaries advance the vision; and the way those two realities merge is through our agreement.*

As mothers, this is an important key in helping progress the calling and destiny of our children. We must work with those we are influencing and encourage the restraints attached to the vision so they can fully walk the path they were made for.

Activating the Prophetic

Finally, prophetic vision reveals our path to destiny and keeps us focused on what we have permission for and what we don't so that each of us can obtain the promise. God's part is to release the vision. Our part is to agree and actively partner with the vision and put the restraints in place in our lives for that vision to be made manifest. Vision *compels* us to stay on our pathway.

Years ago, I started getting prophetic words about speaking and teaching. These words created a new pathway for me that I had to choose to walk on. I had to allow the restraints of that vision to define my season in order for me to reach the destined promise. Practically, I partnered with that word by buying some books about speaking, connecting, and communicating with an audience. I took classes on teaching and preaching and studied some of the great speakers of our time. I said yes to speaking opportunities no matter how small or big, even if I didn't feel qualified or prepared for them. These trainings, books, classes, mentoring, and opportunities all created a new mindset of restraints that I allowed in my life so that I could continue to train and keep on the path towards becoming a powerful speaker and teacher. But, I first had to *agree* with the vision and the restraints in order to get the prize. It was not enough for me to collect prophetic words about speaking and teaching or even to know what needed to be done in order to grow in those areas. To stop there is like being given a car but never learning how to drive it. Until you agree and activate the vision, you're still not moving

> *We put feet to the vision by taking action towards fulfilling it.*

forward. We put feet to the vision by taking action towards fulfilling it.

As we move forward with learning to value the prophetic vision and then activating it in our own lives as well as our sons' and daughters' lives, we must be careful not to judge others for behaviors that demonstrate a lack of vision. How can we judge or rebuke those who are running wild when they haven't been shown the true vision and purpose for their lives? They have nothing to look forward to, no substance of vision to agree with, no words of life or heavenly identity to cling to. God's heart is not to condemn the lost, but to save all who would come to Jesus.

"For God did not send his Son into the world to condemn the world, but to save the world through Him."

John 3:17

What people need is someone to tell them who they are, and mothers are uniquely equipped to do this. Release the prophetic vision that gives purpose, and let the vision be a catalyst to propel those we are influencing into what they were created for. Valuing vision will help us learn to treasure it even more which, as we will see in the next few chapters, is a primary key to walking out our Kingdom assignment.

CHAPTER 7

KEEPING THE VISION ALIVE

GOD GENEROUSLY POURED His Spirit out so that each one of us could be the powerful sons and daughters we were designed to be—that design He saw in His own imagination from the foundations of the earth. Did you know that? *You* were created from God's imagination! You were *His* vision which He has been treasuring for thousands of years looking forward to the day when He would see you brought forth into the earth. He has been longing to see you show up and be all you were created to be in this day, in this time, in this epoch of the world. *You are God's vision.* And just as we treasure the vision we carry for our own children to fulfill everything

> *You are God's vision.*

they are called to be, He is doing the same for each one of us. He is treasuring His own vision for each one of us and is relentless in His great love to see His good plans and purposes unfold in our lives.

"For I know the plans I have for you. Plans to prosper you and not to harm you. Plans to give you a hope and a future."

Jeremiah 29:11

Each of us has our own unique and powerful purpose to fulfill in our generation. Just like King David, who the Bible tells us *"served the purpose of God in his own generation,"*[22] we all are created for a purpose and destiny in Him, and God is affirming the vision He has for you until you become what He sees.

Mary's Treasure

> One of the primary ways a mother owns her assignment begins with affirming the prophetic vision over her children's life.

One of the primary ways a mother owns her assignment begins with affirming the prophetic vision over her children's life. Mary, the mother of Jesus, modeled this value of affirming the vision so well for us. Let me set the stage for you visually. She was with her husband, Joseph, in Bethlehem recovering from labor and delivery in a stable with livestock animals. Somewhere in the fields nearby, a host of angels appeared to some shepherds and announced a powerful prophetic declaration.

---

22   Acts 13:36

"Do not be afraid. I bring you good news that will cause great joy for all the people. Today in the town of David a Savior has been born to you; he is the Messiah, the Lord. This will be a sign to you: You will find a baby wrapped in cloths and lying in a manger."

Luke 2:11-12

The angel proclaimed to the shepherds that a child had been born who is the prophetically-promised, long-awaited Messiah, and that His very arrival on earth would bring about great joy for all of mankind. Then the angel gave directions on where to find this child. I realize this is a familiar story for many, but I want you to catch something here. Mary is recuperating from childbirth in a stable of all places, probably gazing in wonder at this newborn child and recalling the unusual events that had already surrounded His inception and birth. Suddenly, out-of-the-blue, random shepherds come to them and recount the incredible angelic encounter they had just experienced in the fields. Then, once the shepherds confirmed the baby's location and birth as spoken of by the angels, they went out into the region and spread the word about all that they had seen and heard.

"...and all who heard it were amazed at what the shepherds said to them. ***But Mary treasured up all these things and pondered them in her heart."***

Luke 2:19 (emphasis added)

While all who heard the testimony of the shepherds were in awe and amazed, the Bible tells us that Mary, the mother of this helpless baby, *treasured* these things—the prophetic vision released by the angels—and considered them in her heart. The word "treasured" in the original Greek is the word *syntereo* which is defined as *"to keep within one's self, keep in mind (a thing, lest it be forgotten)."* Mary could have easily been lost in amazement with the rest of the crowd and then moved on with her life, not allowing the vision to take root in her heart. But she didn't let the glory or even the largeness of the prophetic vision become lost. She recognized the vision as invaluable and, thus, appropriately *affirmed* the vision by treasuring it until its time of maturity.

To treasure literally means that we, as mothers, keep the vision before us and preserve it at all costs lest the vision become lost or forgotten. This means that no matter what the outward circumstances of our children's lives looks like, the vision must be preserved in the forefront of our hearts because if the vision is lost, so is the possibility for it to be realized.

When I was pregnant with my youngest daughter, there was a prophetic vision of Psalm 91 over her life that she would be protected and no harm would come to her. I remember thinking at the time I received the word, *"Why would I need that Scripture promise for her life?"* Fast-forward to when she was three years old and she suffered an extreme, life-threatening case of pneumonia which put her in a children's hospital for six weeks. The first two weeks of her sickness were the most perilous. Doctors and nurses gravely told me every day that she was not improving and, in fact, her condition was worsening. I cannot express with words how I was feeling as I looked helplessly at my baby girl struggling to breathe, not eating and sleeping for days. These types of trials are precisely the moments when what you believe about God and who He is comes to the forefront, and it is either strengthened or derailed.

Do you know what helped me hold on to hope during that time? It was the fact that God had *already* promised me through the prophetic word I had been given for her years earlier that her life would not be overtaken by a plague, pestilence, or in this case, pneumonia. Because of the prophetic vision, I could not allow the external negative circumstances to supersede God's vision for her life, so I declared His promise over her and kept what He said as my lens rather than what the doctors said. As mothers, we affirm the vision by preserving it until we see it come forth in our children's lives regardless of current events.

Remember, according to Proverbs, without vision people will lead purposeless lives, so one of our responsibilities as mothers is to vigilantly keep the vision alive by treasuring it close so it is never forgotten.

Look To See

There are prophetic visions all around us and within those we are mothering that are continuously being revealed to those who know how to actively *look to see*. When

Moses was in the desert shepherding his father-in-law's sheep, there was a burning bush that caught his eye. I am sure Moses had seen lots of burning bushes in his shepherding career in the desert, but there was something that struck him uniquely about this one. He recognized it as being different than a typical burning bush, and the Bible tells us *"he turned aside to see."*[23]

I propose that God metaphorically has "burning bushes" all around us by which He is trying to get our attention to see and encounter Him in a new way. He is constantly speaking through various means, and our responsibility is to turn aside to look. We must not allow ourselves to be distracted by what's *not* happening in our children's lives and *look to see* what God *is* saying. What God says always trumps what we see.

> *What God says always trumps what we see.*

> *"I will stand at my watch and station myself on the ramparts; I will **look to see** what He will say to me."*
>
> *Habakkuk 2:1 (emphasis added)*

Mothers station themselves within their place of influence and continually *look to see* what God is speaking because they understand that without the vision, their children will never become the world-changers they were born to be. Practically, we can steward this ability to *look to see* in a variety of ways.

---

23   Exodus 3:3

Going After It

You may be asking, how can I affirm the vision if I don't even know what it is? How do I treasure a heavenly identity when I don't know how to find it? Well, based on the outpouring of God's Spirit and the reality that prophetic vision is already accessible to all who believe, there are two principle ways we can discern prophetic vision. Let's begin by looking at Mary, the mother of Jesus, and some other biblical mothers.

The first way to obtain vision is when we personally receive prophetic words for those we are mothering either from the Lord directly or through other people. When the shepherds approached Mary and Joseph and recounted what the angels had told them about Jesus, they were re-laying a prophetic word they had received about Jesus to his parents. We can absolutely receive prophetic words for our children from others around us. Remember though, it is our responsibility to judge the words as to whether they are from God,[24] but receiving from others is a viable way to obtain prophetic vision.

Rebekah, the wife of the patriarch Isaac and mother of Jacob and Esau, received a prophetic word over the twin boys she was carrying. In her case, God spoke to her directly. She personally received a prophetic word from the Lord who told her what their individual futures would look like. He prophesied to her that *"the older shall serve*

---

24   I Corinthians 14:29

the younger."[25] Knowing God's vision for her children's lives, I am sure Rebekah was extremely keen on wanting to know which child would be born first so that she could partner with God's vision for each son. Why did the Lord give this prophetic insight to Rebekah instead of Isaac? I believe it's connected to a mother's particular assignment in her children's lives. As mothers, once we have judged and processed a prophetic word to be from God, it is our responsibility to keep the vision in our hearts and minds as we raise up our sons and daughters.

It's been twelve years that I've been treasuring my youngest daughter's prophetic word that she would be a trail-blazer and would have an audience one day. Just recently at a prophetic conference at my home church, she received another prophetic word that clarified and expanded the original one we received for her. Kris Vallotton, a prophet and teacher from Bethel Church, had a word of knowledge for someone's daughter named "Elli," and we were the only ones in a room of a thousand people who had a daughter named Elli. He proceeded to prophesy about her role in creativity and saw her doing evangelistic productions similar to what the healing evangelist Aimee Semple-McPherson used to do. That was especially meaningful to me since my paternal grandparents and great-grandmother were all ordained under Aimee's powerful ministry. That prophetic word given by Kris felt like it was not just a destiny word for my daughter but a her-

---

25   Genesis 25:23

itage word as well. As a mother, I received this prophetic word from another person because I judged it to be true and consistent with Scripture, the nature of God, and other words and promises Elli has received.

Remember, according to the Book of Joel, we are all equipped to hear God's voice, and one of the first points of reference to receive prophetic vision for your children is *you*! God wants to speak to you about those whom you are mothering. He has heavenly se-crets about your children's iden-tities and purposes that He is longing to reveal. As a mother, you are particularly equipped to be in tune to God's voice to identify His vision for their lives.

> *As a mother, you are particularly equipped to be in tune to God's voice to identify His vision for their lives.*

Gifts Reveal Vision

The second way we can obtain vision for our children is by looking at the gifts that are already in them. The Lord often speaks a vision for our sons and daughters through His word, but He has also *already* spoken about who they are through the gifts He has placed in their lives since their very inception. Biblically and in the world around us, we find that mothers have a unique ability to recognize the needs, giftings, and callings in their children's lives. Practi-cally, this "mother's intuition" is as simple as paying atten-tion to and watching for the gifts to manifest themselves as our children grow naturally and spiritually.

As a young boy, my brother had a strong entrepreneurial gift that became more evident the older he got. Whether it was offering to sell homemade lemonade at our neighborhood corner or mowing lawns around the neighborhood, he would often look for creative ways to earn money. As an adult, we saw the seeds of that gift grow into full maturity as he started and ran a very successful vacation rental business that he eventually sold for a great profit. Additionally, he would mentor others by teaching them how to run their own profitable Kingdom business. My brother became a successful businessman as an adult, but the entrepreneurial and teaching gifts he carried that contributed to his success were already inside of him as a child. We can often see the seeds of destiny in our sons and daughters if we *look to see* them.

Mary experienced this recognition of gifts when twelve-year-old Jesus went seemingly missing for three days as they were traveling out of Jerusalem. Jesus' parents rushed back to Jerusalem in search of Him. He was finally found in the temple where He was dialoguing with the rabbis and teachers astounding all who heard Him because of the wisdom He carried. His response to His parents when they finally found Him was along the lines of, *"How could you not know where I would be? I am about my Father's business."* Essentially, Jesus was reminding them that He was put on the earth for a purpose and that they should have recognized that His gifts and calling were all leading Him towards that purpose.

The Bible records that Mary responded once again by treasuring these things in her heart.[26]

When my son was a very young toddler, he did what every young child does; he made lots and lots of noise. He would usually clutch a toy in his hand and start banging on a table, furniture, the floor, or anything that would make a loud sound when he hit it. Obviously, too many loud noises can drive you crazy as a parent, but I noticed something different with him. Whenever he struck something, there was a rhythm to it, a pattern. There was an intentional sound, almost like he was trying to recreate a sound on the outside that he heard internally. I realized then that he had been given a gift of rhythm, and I began watching for opportunities to see that gift grow and mature.

God has placed gifts inside every single person on the planet that He will never remove or take back. This is why it says,

> *"Each of you should use whatever gift you have received to serve others..."*
>
> *1 Peter 4:10*

and,

> *"...for God's gifts and His call are irrevocable."*
>
> *Romans 11:29*

How and whether people choose to operate and steward these gifts is up to each individual, yet His desire is to

---

26 Luke 2:51

see every son and daughter come into their fullest expression of themselves. Their gifts are a significant part of that.

Practical Prophecy

On their birthdays, I ask the Lord for prophetic insight concerning each of my children. I spend time with the Lord and ask what He is saying about each one—where they are at internally, what season they are in, and what I should look for and connect with in the next year. I love reflecting on these words after the year has gone by because I can see His faithfulness in speaking to me and can rejoice in how I was able to intentionally connect with my children in ways that were meaningful to them.

Another practical thing I do is speak prophetically over my children according to their names. Because a name can reveal identity and destiny, every time we use our children's names, it's as though we are prophesying over them. My son Ethan's name means, "strong and steadfast." As a mother, I continually remind him that God has created him to be strong so that he can help those who are weak and be a defender to the defenseless. We also named him Ethan after one of the chief musicians and worship leaders in David's Tabernacle.[27] Therefore, in naming him, I am prophesying that he has a destiny in worship, wisdom and leadership. All of these are practical mothering ways I have discovered in order to partner with the Lord's vision over my children's lives.

---

27   I Chronicles 15:17,19

Another way to gather prophetic words for your children is to connect with a prophetic community near you and simply ask others to prophesy over them. I would suggest that you record these words on your phone so you can transcribe it later. You can also ask those you are spiritually mothering for copies of the prophetic words they've received so you can start praying into and agreeing with their heavenly identity. Many churches have prophetic teams where you can set up an appointment to be ministered prophetically to and receive encouragement. Go after the prophetic vision! It is God's delight to bring forth the vision at the appointed time. It will never delay and is always available to those who seek for it like the treasure it is.[28]

Affirming the vision given on behalf of our children, practicing our ability to hear the Lord's voice over them, and choosing to *look to see* what unique gifts they have are all significant keys in our assignment to raise up world-changers. Next, we will delve into how mothers are uniquely wired to strengthen, encourage, and comfort others into their destiny.

---

28 Habakkuk 2:3

CHAPTER 8

ASSISTING THE VISION

O NCE WE HAVE LEARNED to identify, value, and treasure the prophetic vision over our children's lives,
we must move into assisting the vision to see it come forth.
Practically and prophetically, the steps to coming alongside any vision can be found in the the Book of First Corinthians.

> *"But the one who prophesies speaks to people for their*
> *strengthening, encouraging and comfort."*
>
> *I Corinthians 14:3*

In the context of our assignment, we find that mothers are uniquely gifted and equipped to come alongside
to strengthen, encourage, and comfort those they are influencing until they become the mighty ones we see
them to be.

Strengthen

The first part of the nature of a mother is connected to the first part of the nature of the pro- phetic. Strength. Mothers lend strength to those we are lead- ing until they find their own strength. We find this particular

> *Mothers lend strength to those we are leading until they find their own strength.*

grace demonstrated for us in the Book of Judges through the prophetess Deborah, Israel's only female judge, who was also known as the "mother of Israel."[29] Here was a mother who was raising a nation of world-changers, and we can learn much from her.

The fourth chapter of Judges reports that during the time of her ruling, the nation of Israel was once again in the seemingly endless cycle of oppression. At this time, the oppression has lasted twenty years. The Lord spoke to Deborah to go to war against the evil commander Si- sera and his army who were oppressive enemies of Israel. She summoned Israel's General Barak and commissioned him to fulfill the task. She made it pretty easy for him, too, by laying out blueprints of the war plan, instructing how many troops to take, and sharing what the Lord's intention and outcome would be that would ultimately make Israel victorious. Yet, notice Barak's response to Deborah and her own dialogue in reply to him:

---

29 Judges 5:7

> *"Barak said to her, 'If you will go with me, I will go.*
> *But if you will not go with me, I will not go.' 'I will gladly*
> *go with you,' she said, 'but you will receive no honor on*
> *the road you are about to take, because the Lord will sell*
> *Sisera to a woman.' So Deborah got up and went with*
> *Barak to Kedesh."*
>
> *Judges 4:8-9*

Barak needed Deborah's strength to go with him. She released him to soar on his own, yet he was in a place in his process where he needed her strength alongside him in order for him to feel he could be successful. He needed the strength of the *mother of Israel* to go to war and to feel confident in the outcome.

I believe Deborah had a prophetic vision of Barak that was far greater than he saw for himself, and she was calling him up into that reality even though he apparently didn't feel ready for it. This is part of our assignment. Mothers lend strength to others until they can see themselves the way we see them. We are called to have vision for our children, but we also understand that everyone is in process and each of our sons and daughters have their own journey to take toward being the world-changers they were created to be. This is where the prophetic nature of a mother comes in.

> *Mothers lend strength to others until they can see themselves the way we see them.*

We lend our strength to them until they are strong enough and know they can do it themselves.

My sister, Heather, is a powerful worship leader who leads a worship movement in San Diego, California, called One Sound. During a session she was teaching in a worship school, ministry and prayer began to break out. A young woman who had been suffering with back pain for several years was in the session, and my sister asked if they (my sister and her son) could pray for her. After they prayed for her, there was a significant decrease in the pain, and she felt so encouraged! The woman then relayed to my sister that she had received prophetic words about having healing hands but had never healed anyone before. So my sister, being the anointed prophetic mother she is, asked the woman if she wanted to activate those prophetic words right then.

She asked the young woman, *"How would you like to heal at the meeting tonight?"* The young woman nervously agreed. So my sister invited anyone in the room who had back pain to come forward. She told those who responded that this young woman would pray for them, and they would receive healing. Jesus tells us in the Book of Matthew, *"Freely you have received, freely give,"*[30] and so this woman who had freely received healing in her own back was now about to release the same healing to others. As people came forward, the young woman walked up to them, put her hands on them, and prayed this simple prayer,

30   Matthew 10:8

"Healing come. Pain go. In Jesus name." As she was praying, my sister stood behind this young woman with her hand on her back lending her own strength and faith so she knew she was not alone. When the young lady moved down the line, Heather moved along with her ever keeping her hand on this woman's back releasing strength. Heather stayed with the young woman until everyone was prayed for! Even more than the healings that took place that evening, what impacted and will remain with this young lady forever was how my sister lent her own strength so she could take her first steps in healing with confidence.

> *Mothers lend their strength until the battle is won.*

Mothers lend their strength until the battle is won. We look into the eyes of those we are raising up and declare to them, *"You can do this! You've got this! You were made to shine in this moment, and I will make sure you feel my strength until you taste your victory,"* just like Deborah did for Barak and just like Heather did for this young woman.

For seven years I oversaw the small Christian school that my children attended. It was a wonderful school that had been running for thirty years and had changed many lives including my own(I was employed as a junior high teacher right out of Bible college there). However, due to financial and logistical reasons, the school ceased to exist right around the time my children were old enough to attend it. Because of a personal value and conviction I had for Christian education, I felt a grace to keep this school up and running, not only for my own children's sake but for the future children who would benefit from the school. I carried and communicated the vision, hired teachers, and connected with families to build this school from three students to a place where we had three full-time teachers and a part-time office staff.

During that time, we hired a young couple. I saw a grace on their lives to be not just teachers but the school's headmasters as well. As I developed more of a relationship with them and saw their outstanding character, I had a prophetic vision of "passing the baton" of the school's leadership to them. As a result of this vision, all of my interactions with them were to show them what I knew regarding operating the school. I modeled for them how to manage certain responsibilities associated with running the school and then gave them smaller tasks to help grow their confidence. I watched how they connected with parents and teachers and offered counsel and my strength whenever they encountered an uncertain situation. I slowly gave them more of the reins until they were confident and strong enough to carry the oversight of the school completely. Good mothers desire for their children to be successful, and my heart was to see this young couple thrive in their calling. Eventually, I did hand over the leadership of the school to them, and they did a wonderful job of stewarding what was given them. The point is this: The vision caused me to look at them with the end goal in mind and mother them accordingly.

Many know that Thomas Edison, who has been described as America's greatest inventor, is credited with making a long-lasting, practical, working electric light bulb available to the world, changing forever life as it was then known. Interestingly, he also invented the phonograph, the motion picture camera, and was *"one of the first inventors to apply the principles of mass production and teamwork to the process of invention."*[31] Much of what was once thought impossible for thousands of years, we now consider necessities in our generation, and we owe them to this man.

Edison was a world-changer in the literal sense of the word, but it didn't come easy for him. As a young boy, he was labeled and identified as "mentally ill or incompetent" by his teachers, though many now believe he may have been dyslexic or had some sort of learning disorder which had not been diagnosed at the time. Instead of listening to the teacher and stopping his education, his mother, Nancy Edison, a formal school teacher herself who was not employed at the time so she could raise her own children, decided to homeschool her son. As a mother, she did not see the lack in her son's ability to learn as an obstacle. She took the opportunity to lend her own strength to him until he was able to soar himself. As history plays out, soar he did. Thomas said this about her: *"My mother was the making of me. She was so sure of me; and I felt I had something to live for, someone I must not disappoint."*[32]

---

31 https://en.m.wikipedia.org/wiki/Thomas_Edison

32 https://www.nps.gov/edis/learn/historyculture/samuel-and-nancy-elliott-edison.htm

Encourage

The second piece to the prophetic nature of a mother is encouragement. The word encouragement literally means to *"fill with courage."* As we continue to treasure prophetic vision for our children and strengthen them along the way by lending our own strength when it's needed, we also need to fuel our children with the courage necessary to be who they are. Being a world-changer is not for the faint of heart, and in order to fully embrace all they are created for, they must continually be filled with courage.

I have been a worship director for twenty years, and I've come to realize that my function is not just as a worship leader. I am mothering our worship community as well. When I first moved to my home church, The Mission in Vacaville, California, and accepted the worship director position, there had been quite a shift in the worship department with almost all of the primary worship leaders either moving out of the area or stepping down for a season to pursue other areas of calling and passion. This exodus of almost all of our worship leaders left a massive gap in our worship community for a short season. As I took inventory of who was left, I discovered several "hidden gems" who were anointed and only needed the opportunity and permission to grow as powerful worship leaders themselves. They needed someone to fill them with courage. So that first year after my arrival, I began intentionally partnering with each potential leader. They co-led with me so they could learn what it feels like to lead others in freedom and find that they, too, had permission to be themselves in worship. My heart was to lend my strength and fuel them with courage until they could feel more confident as they learned to be the best version of themselves in their unique calling. Now each of those co-leaders is leading on their own powerfully, releasing their own sound consistent with who they uniquely are. Mothers remind children of who they are and fill them with courage and boldness until they can soar for themselves.

> *Mothers remind children of who they are and fill them with courage and boldness until they can soar for themselves.*

Deborah was considered the "mother of Israel" because she was raising a nation of world-changers, and she was able to release the strength that was uniquely hers. She didn't shrink back in fear when Israel needed a champion. Rather, she said yes to the Lord and boldly stepped into her own assignment of being a mother to a nation. As a result, the Bible records that Israel was saved and had peace for forty years.[33] While I believe all women are called to mother others at some point, there are some who are called to mother a nation or even many nations. They will completely step into the responsibility of motherhood and strengthen a nation to be who God called them to be.

Heidi Baker is one of those world-changing women who is a mother not only of the nation of Mozambique,

---

33 Judges 5:31

Africa, but an entire world-wide generation of lovers of God. By her example and encouragement, multitudes of people around the globe are finding the courage to love God without reservation. We are all made for this kind of fearless love, and Heidi has mothered so well in encouragement toward that end.

Comfort

Comfort is the third attribute in the nature of a mother and the trait which is attributed to mothers probably more than any other. When a child falls down and gets hurt or is in great need, who do they run to for comfort? They usually run to mom. While the term *comfort* is synonymous with consolation, there are a few other definitions listed in the Greek dictionary for the word that is translated as "comfort" in our text passage which I would like to share with you. When we are told that prophecy is to *"strengthen, encourage, and comfort,"* the word for comfort here in the original Greek is *paramytheia* which is defined not just as consolation but also *to persuade* and *to stimulate*. In the context of our assignment, mothers also comfort their children by persuading them of who they are. They comfort them by stimulating them to greater vision of who they are. When anyone catches heaven's vision for their life, that revelation brings comfort. Every time I feel challenged about my identity or my lack of qualifications in a particular area, there is a tremendous amount of comfort I find in the Lord when He reminds me of who I am. This comfort allows me to recalibrate to His truth so I can then function from His grace.

At a particular moment in the world-wide blockbuster movie, *The Black Panther*, the Lord spoke so strongly to me through the storyline that it hit my spirit like a hammer. The story is set around a young African prince who is called to lead his powerful nation after his father, the king, is killed. However, the nation's law had a provision where any noble prince from another tribe could come and challenge the right to the throne by fighting until one of the contending princes surrenders. In one particular scene, our hero is fighting another tribal prince who challenged him for the throne, and it looked for a few nail-biting minutes that the rightful heir could be losing the battle. We see his head roll backward after a targeted punch to the face. As the camera zooms in through his perspective, we see his eyes focus on the queen, his mother. He sees her mouth move as she yells out to him, *"Show him who you are!"* In that moment, the young hero remembers who he is, and his head snaps back up to continue the battle—only now he is fighting like the king he is. He defeats the challenger and is able to take his rightful place as king of the nation.

> *Mothers comfort their children by reminding them of who they are.*

Mothers comfort their children by reminding them of who they are. Sometimes that can be a challenge because it can seem we are daily faced with who they are not. Nevertheless, our assignment requires us to remind our sons and daughters of who they are. This is why treasuring the prophetic vision is so important at the foundation. Holding the vision at the forefront allows *us* to remember who they are so that we can continue to encourage and remind *them* of who they are until what we see in them is what they see in themselves.

My oldest daughter, Faith, is just like her name. She's strong, fearless, and powerful. There is no obstacle in her way, which can be great yet occasionally challenging as a mother. Saying "no" to a daughter with that kind of confidence most of the time results in her finding another way to get what she wants(she *may* be a tiny bit like her mother).

When she was a toddler, we ran mommy/daughter errands together. When we ran into friends at the local grocery store or library, I introduced her to them, "*Faith, this is so-and-so, can you say hi to them?*" At which point, she would defiantly turn her face away and make a grunting noise that communicated quite strongly, "*NO, I will not!*" While I have no problem with my child acting imperfect in front of friends or strangers, this felt unacceptably rude, and I knew I needed to go after this with her.

Privately, I coached her that when mommy introduces you to someone, the kind thing to do is to greet them back. She then informed me that the reason she couldn't do that is she was shy. "*I shy, Mommy. I shy,*" she would say in her little three-year old voice. Now, I had a choice to make here. I certainly didn't want to force my daughter to greet every person I connect with, but I also couldn't let her believe and adapt as a personality trait that she was shy. Shy is a lie from the enemy, and I wasn't going to allow my daughter to be its prey. So, I encouraged her, *"You are not shy, Faith. You have the Lion of the Tribe of Judah living within you, and you are as bold and courageous as a lion."* Each time she would say she was shy, I would tell her this truth about herself. I reminded her of the truth of who she was. I'm not sure how long it took, but I remember there was a shift at some point where she stopped turning away from people and began greeting them. I never heard her speak "shy" over herself again.

Today, as a teenager, Faith is a social and fearless young woman when meeting new people and making friends—way more than my other two children. As a mother, I saw an opportunity to displace a lie by replacing it with the truth of who she was. I spoke the truth until I saw it manifested in her life, and today you would never know she struggled with shyness as a young girl. This is the powerful kind of comfort that mothers give. Mothers release comfort by persuading and awakening their charges to the reality of who they are.

> *Mothers release comfort by persuading and awakening their charges to the reality of who they are.*

In the Book of Exodus, we find the story of a fearless mother named Jochabed, a Hebrew woman living in Egypt who had the unfortunate reality of being pregnant with a son. It was unfortunate because every Hebrew boy born in that period of time was commanded by Pharaoh to be murdered. As she looked upon her son, we find an interesting exchange:

> *"When she saw that he was a fine child, she hid him for three months. But when she could hide him no longer, she got a papyrus basket for him...she placed the child in it and put it among the reeds along the bank of the Nile. His sister stood at a distance to see what would happen to him."*

> *Exodus 2:2-4*

Jochabed risked her life because she saw something unique about her son who we know became the powerful biblical character Moses, God's chosen deliverer. You could almost say this mother had a "prophetic vision" for Moses' life, and that revelation gave her courage to defy the governmental laws of her day so that her son could live out his fullest potential. *How* she knew he was special or beautiful, the Bible isn't clear on, but there was something about Moses that caused her to utilize her own strength, courage, and comfort as a mother to come alongside Moses' own helpless frame until he could grow and become the great deliverer of Israel as well as the author of the first five books of the Old Testament. Just as Jochabed assisted her son at a time when he had no capacity for those things, we have the privilege and assignment to do the same.

Because the very nature of the prophetic as seen in First Corinthians 14:3 is to strengthen, encourage, and comfort, it is along those values that we must choose to agree and assist the vision in those whom we are impacting. Once again, will people step into all they are called to be without the prophetic nature and support of Kingdom mothers? It's possible, but I believe the Lord has intentionally placed the family dynamic in His Body so that we can avoid much pain, purposelessness, and discouragement in the journey towards becoming mighty. Inviting mothers and fathers into your process will accelerate your destiny and give you the strength, courage, and comfort you need to fulfill all you were called to be.

CHAPTER 9

ACCELERATING DESTINY'S

W E ALL CARRY SEEDS within us to be a blessing to the world around us. Remember, we are blessed to be a blessing; everything we receive is to ultimately be given. We see this beautifully displayed in the final key of our assignment. Since Mary, the mother of Jesus, was one of our primary inspirations for understanding the assignment of motherhood, let's go back to her story and watch this final key unfold.

We all carry seeds within us to be a blessing to the world around us.

As we have watched Jesus through her eyes, we have seen from His inception, birth, and growth that Mary treasured the vision of the prophetic promises over His life. Remember, by treasuring the prophetic vision for Jesus, she consistently kept those promises right in front of her, not letting them out of her sight. Throughout His years, we can presume that she was always keeping an eye out for how she could strengthen, encourage, and comfort Him towards His destiny.

This ability to continually treasure and hold the vision in the forefront helps us as mothers to recognize those moments when our children have an opportunity to step into their destinies. That is just what Mary did for Jesus. Did you know that it was Jesus' mother who first activated His public ministry? It all began at a wedding. This is a longer passage that is worth reading through because I want you to catch the interaction between Jesus and His mother here.

"On the third day a wedding took place at Cana in Galilee. Jesus' mother was there, and Jesus and His disciples had also been invited to the wedding. When the wine was gone, Jesus' mother said to Him, 'They have no more wine.' 'Woman, why do you involve me?' Jesus replied, 'My hour has not yet come.' His mother said to the servants, 'Do whatever he tells you.' Nearby stood six stone water jars, the kind used by the Jews for ceremonial washing, each holding from twenty to thirty gallons. Jesus said to the servants, 'Fill the jars with water'; so they filled them to the brim. Then He told them, 'Now draw some out and take it to the master of the banquet.' They did so, and the master of the banquet tasted the water that had been turned into wine. He did not realize where it had come from, though the servants who had drawn the water knew. Then he called the bridegroom aside and said, 'Everyone brings out the choice wine first and then

the cheaper wine after the guests have had too much to drink; but you have saved the best till now.'"

John 2:1-10

There is so much in this story that could be fun to unpack, but one of the first questions we should ask is how did Mary even know Jesus could *do* that? How did she know He could turn water into wine? I agree with what Kris Vallotton says: *"It's probably because it wasn't the first time He had executed that marvel."* Mary obviously had confidence in His ability to perform a miracle and, in particular, this ability to transform one substance into a completely different one. Why would she have been so confident in what He could do in public unless she had first seen His power displayed in private as He grew up?

The first lesson about acceleration that we can learn from this portion of the story is that as we treasure the vision and support the gifts and calling in our children, we must be aware of how those whom we are influencing are stewarding their own vision. For example, my oldest daughter has a vision to play soccer in Brazil some day. She is an excellent soccer player and has been a part of many award-winning soccer teams. But for her to accomplish her dream of being invited to play in the nation of Brazil, she must steward what she is currently doing in soccer. She has to strengthen her ball handling skills, increase her running stamina, and do this every day for a long time to even be considered good enough to play in another country.

> *We can do everything as mothers to help our children be successful, but ultimately it is their choice to believe and step into that reality for themselves.*

We have to crawl before we can walk. We have to walk before we can run. At the end of the day, no one can make you do anything; you are responsible for you. We can do everything as mothers to help our children be successful, but ultimately it is their choice to believe and step into that reality for themselves. I believe Mary had personal experience observing Jesus doing signs and wonders as He developed, and she knew He was ready for this public challenge.

As a mother, if I had my son play drums on our Sunday morning worship band when he hadn't shown any interest in practicing drums in private, then I would be doing him a disservice that could have negative consequences for himself, the band, and the congregation. Mary knew Jesus was more than capable to perform this miracle publicly because of what she had seen Him steward privately. Mothers watch for their children to take ownership of their own calling and then look for opportunities and seasons to activate it appropriately.

> *Mothers watch for their children to take ownership of their own calling and then look for opportunities and seasons to activate it appropriately.*

There are many wonderful and anointed worship leaders within the worship community I oversee. As the leader who is currently mothering this amazing tribe of people, I am always watching to see who is managing their anointing well. I'm observing whose "yes" means "yes" as well as who frequently commits but doesn't follow through as promised. Who is ready to steward their anointing to the next level by being teachable and taking advantage of the local resources we have available to grow their gift? There are some on my team who perhaps aren't the most-seasoned musicians, but their faithfulness day in and day out has increased their favor. When a big opportunity arises, I know who to promote because I've observed how they have stewarded their gifting and calling. I know I can count on them because I've watched them in private. Mothers don't need to idealistically look at their children and think it's all rainbows and unicorns! When it comes to accelerating your children's destinies, a wise mother will have payed attention to whether they are ready or not for promotion.

Back at the wedding in Cana, we find a minor crises unfolding. The wine had run out, and Mary seemed to be concerned about this. We see an interesting exchange between her and Jesus as she appeals to Him to do something about the problem. All she said to Him was, "*They have no more wine.*" Somehow Jesus knew she wasn't just expressing an observation or asking Him to go out and purchase more wine for the party. He understood she was asking Him to do a miracle, thus activating His public ministry.

Look at His response to her request. "*Why do you involve me? My hour has not yet come.*" Essentially, Jesus was telling His sweet tenacious mother that He was not supposed to

reveal who He was with power, signs, and wonders publicly yet. Her response to Him is priceless. I can just envision
her dismissing Him with a wave of her hand as if she didn't
hear Him or couldn't be bothered, and then turning to nearby servants, she commands them, *"Do whatever He says."*
The Bible documents that while on earth as a man, Jesus
did whatever He saw the Father doing. Apparently He also
did what His mama said! As the story unfolds, we see that
Jesus did in fact do what His mother asked and miraculous-
ly changed the water into wine that was described as the

best wine at the wedding. God
never does anything half-hearted or mediocre. When God is
invited and involved, it's always
the best. As we see in Jesus' first
miracle, this was no exception. It
was at this moment, this beginning of miracles, that belief was
activated in His disciples.

> *God never does anything
> half-hearted or mediocre.
> When God is invited
> and involved, it's always
> the best.*

*"What Jesus did here in Cana of Galilee **was the
first of the signs through which he revealed his glory;** and his disciples believed in him."*

John 2:11

This miracle displayed Jesus' power publicly, and it
was His *mother* who accelerated that destiny for Him. He
wasn't ready to do it yet, but He allowed His mother to
pull that future season into the now. God has a special

108

place in His heart for mothers and their prayers. This picture of Jesus listening to His mother and doing what she asked reveals that God has given mothers a unique place and authority to accelerate their children's destinies.

This miracle displayed Jesus' power publicly, and it was His mother who accelerated that destiny for Him.

An Audacious Request

We see this same desire to accelerate destinies in the mother of James and John who were known as the "Sons of Thunder" and were part of Jesus' inner core group of disciples.

> *"Then the mother of Zebedee's sons came to Jesus with her sons and, kneeling down, asked a favor of Him. 'What is it you want?' he asked. She said, 'Grant that one of these two sons of mine may sit at your right and the other at your left in Your kingdom.' 'You don't know what you are asking.' Jesus said to them. 'Can you drink the cup I am going to drink?'"*
>
> *Matthew 20:20-22*

What an audacious request! Only a mother could get away with such a lofty appeal. Notice in the above passage that Jesus did not rebuke James and John's mother for the request. I believe it was because she correctly envisioned that her sons were destined to be rulers with Jesus though she did not understand the vision's application. Jesus Himself confirmed her vision when speaking about His disciples in the Book of Matthew when He mentions they will each sit on twelve thrones with Him at the renewal of all things.

Think about it! James and John's mom had treasured the vision for them, and then she used her influence as their mother to approach Jesus on behalf of her sons, seeking to accelerate their destiny. Mothers do this; we look for opportunities to appropriately use our influence to accelerate the destiny of our children. This is part of raising up world-changers. We don't stop with treasuring the vision nor with guiding it as they grow. We look for opportunities to release our children into their next chapter of glory.

Mothers Creating Opportunities

Let's look at yet another mother in the Bible who modeled this same principle of acceleration. Bathsheba had a promise that her son, Solomon, would be king after David. When that promise was threatened, she took it upon herself to advance that vision by going before King David and reminding him of his promise. And as a result, Solomon was appointed king over Israel that very day.

Naomi, the mother-in-law of Ruth the Moabitess, took it upon herself to accelerate Ruth's destiny by using her own influence to secure a place of safety for her.

110

*"One day Ruth's mother-in-law Naomi said to her,
'My daughter, I must find a home for you, where you will
be well provided for.'"*

Ruth 3:1

It was Naomi's counsel that advanced Ruth's destiny. Consequently Ruth, a Gentile, was eventually included in the lineage of two of the greatest world-changers ever known—King David and Jesus Himself.

The assignment of motherhood does not allow us to be content with anything less than the highest and the best for our children. Mothers utilize their favor to propel, accelerate, and advance the destiny of those they are called to influence.

> *Mothers utilize their favor to propel, accelerate, and advance the destiny of those they are called to influence.*

One of the worship leaders in our community is just an all-around amazing woman. She has the heart of a servant, does everything with a positive attitude, makes things fun, is smart, humble, forward-thinking, and an advancer. On top of it all, she is very anointed in worship. I have had my eye on her for over a year now for a position within our community as my worship administrator. At the time I noticed her, the position was filled, but I had a sense that it would be opening soon. Within about six months, the person holding this position resigned to pursue other dreams, and I jumped on the opportunity to accelerate this young woman's destiny. You see, her *dream* is to serve in worship full time, and the vision I've seen for her life is in tandem with that. She has stewarded her gifts and calling with wisdom and I want to see her thrive and be in a place where she operates to her fullest capacity in the area she loves. So when the position arose, I approached the leaders of the church and recommended her not only as worship administrator but as personal assistant to our senior leader. I used my influence to accelerate hers. After the application and interview process, she was hired, and honestly, our church staff and leadership are already feeling the massive benefits of having her on the team.

Mothers, both naturally and spiritually, will not be satisfied until the vision they have carried and supported is realized and manifested. When the Canaanite woman with the demonized daughter went before Jesus, she knew she had no social right to approach Him for healing. Yet as a mother, she would not allow anything to stand in the way of her daughter's destiny of being free! She went against every social and cultural protocol to tenaciously appeal to Jesus for healing and would not give up or give in until she received what she knew belonged to her child. And you know what? She received her request. Her daughter was healed and delivered.

As mothers, I believe we are particularly good at accelerating destinies. We don't do it because we feel obligated but because it is natural for mothers *to want* to promote those whom they are influencing. Women in particular find a sense of accomplishment in seeing those we love and have mothered go places farther and faster than our own current reality. Because raising world-changers is our assignment, we cannot be content to let our children remain in the safety of preparation. Eventually, if we've done our job,

> *Because raising world-changers is our assignment, we cannot be content to let our children remain in the safety of preparation.*

it will be time for them to soar on their own. The final key in seeing that reality come forth is to use our influence, when appropriate, to accelerate and release our children into their destinies.

PART III

WALKING IN THE ASSIGNMENT

CHAPTER 10

UNDERSTANDING FAMILY DYNAMICS

T HERE ARE SOME IMPORTANT distinctions that need to be understood as we all grow in love and maturity in the family of God, especially as there will come a time when those whom we are mothering will mature and possibly no longer need our mothering voice.

First John 3:1 says, *"See what kind of love the Father has given to us, that we should be called children of God; and so we are."*[34] We are all daughters and sons, and we always will be because God is our Father. Yet it is important to realize that being children of God is how we relate to *Him*! It shouldn't be how we forever relate to one another. There are seasons where we are daughters and sons to some, but eventually we should mature into mothers and fathers. Just as in the natural we begin this life as infants, grow into childhood, and mature into adulthood, there are pathways of growth in Kingdom family.

---

34 ESV

God never meant for us to forever remain as children in our relationships with one another. This is not to say that we will no longer need mothers and fathers in our lives, but rather our relationships with them *should* grow to the point that we eventually benefit from their voice in more of a peer relationship. My spiritual father in adulthood had that place in my life for almost twenty years, but there came a time when I matured to where I no longer needed him for constant advice and approval. I would occasionally call and receive counsel from him, but I had become strong enough to know how to make many decisions on my own without his regular input. There is a vast difference between fathering daughters and fathering mothers.

It happens sometimes that spiritual parents raise their children to be mothers and fathers but then don't make room for them to operate as such in the house. This is a primary issue I have witnessed in life in general, but particularly in the church. Ask any parent of adult children, and they will tell you parenting a son as a child and parenting a son who is now a father himself requires an entirely different approach. Spiritually, we should expect to make this adjustment in our relationships with those we are influencing as they grow and mature. Let's make room for sons to become fathers and daughters to become mothers in the same house. There's always room for more. God's heart is for each of us to mature to the place where we can continually speak to the next generation of His goodness.

"One generation commends your works to another;
they tell of your mighty acts."

Psalm 145:4

In this familial cycle of life and maturity, there should always be three types of Kingdom family relationships active in our lives in order to remain healthy. Identifying these relationships can be determined by asking yourself the following three questions: *Who do I allow to speak into my life as mothers and fathers? Who am I running with as brothers and sisters?* And lastly, *who am I pouring into as my sons and daughters?*

Mothers and Fathers

All of us need mothers and fathers to speak into the vision they see in our lives. One of the ways you can identify those voices in your life is to look at who you are relationally connected to for receiving revelation, counsel, or impartation. There are two markers I have learned to look for over the years that help me choose those who would be given the privilege to speak into my life. I look to see whose well I am drinking from and also whose trees are currently in my field that offered shade as I grow. Let me explain.

King David was a mighty leader who knew how to transform a ragtag group of distressed, indebted, and discontented underdogs into mighty warriors who performed great exploits. In fact, the Bible records that these men would eventually become not just an "average" army, but they would resemble even *the army of God*.[35] What happened here? What was the significant difference in these disillusioned men's lives that transformed them into world-changers? The answer is found in who they chose to serve. They knew that if they wanted to kill giants, they needed to follow a giant-killer. To become great, they needed to serve someone great. If you want to be a world-changer, follow world-changers.

> *"These four Philistines were descendants of the giants of Gath, but David **and his warriors** killed them."*
>
> II Samuel 21:22 (NLT)

Personally, as I seek out fathers and mothers, I look for those who are carrying something I need or desire for my own life or call. Who are the ones who have taken ground in an area I am needing breakthrough in and trying to possess? Who are the ones who have killed "giants" in a particular sphere that I need to advance in, and how do I follow their example? Who you surround yourself with, you become like.

Who you surround yourself with, you become like.

> *"Walk with the wise and become wise, for a companion of fools suffers harm."*
>
> Proverbs 13:20

---

35   I Chronicles 12:22

Identify those who are living where you want to live and pursue their voice in your life whether personal or distant. Bill Johnson and Heidi Baker have both greatly impacted my life personally and are both modeling what fathering and mothering is to an entire generation they have never met by the way they live and the messages they release. Their books, teachings, and resources on Kingdom and the love of God have all transformed me. The fruit of their ministries and lives have influenced me, yet I have never spent more than a few seconds with either of them. Eric Stovesand, a man you have probably never heard of, spiritually fathered me as an adult for over twenty years. His empowering ways spoken personally into my life and into particular situations absolutely shaped and transformed me. Two global leaders I have no intimate connection with and one local leader I was in contact with weekly all mothered and fathered me in certain ways and seasons. Look for those from whose well you are drinking, and don't stop until you grow into the fullness of everything God has for you that is contained in that relationship.

> *Look for those from whose well you are drinking, and don't stop until you grow into the fullness of everything God has for you that is contained in that relationship.*

Secondly, mothers and fathers will champion a greater vision for your life than even you can see. I love what Cleddie Keith says, *"Never put yourself under the leadership of someone who doesn't have a greater vision for your life than you have for your own."*

Sometimes there are seasons when you are assigned to authority that can be difficult and challenging, like David with King Saul. Though Saul tried several times to kill David, David never allowed the challenge to hinder who he was and what he was called to do. David stayed true to his desire to honor Saul, and he continued to make attempts at peace with him. At the same time, David would not let Saul's opinion of him derail his assignment.

There may be occasions when you find yourself serving a leader who is not necessarily a mother or father to you. At times, I served leaders under whom I felt I had to fight to be who I was called to be. In one particular situation, as a leader and a woman, the unspoken message I received from leadership was that I was temporarily "filling in the gap" until a man could come and fill my position. Even though I knew I was God's choice for that season, I had to learn how to honor and not be offended, even when the season changed.

In another situation, I encountered a leader who attempted to use their position to take control of an enterprise I had founded and been successfully running for quite some time. It was challenging because my heart is always to honor leaders, but at the same time, I knew in this case they were wrong. I knew there was a way to stay true to my assignment while honoring this leader's position at the same time. The challenge certainly put me in a difficult place, and I had to make some hard decisions. Thankfully, through God's grace, He made a way that released me and this leader with no damage.

Though each of these leaders had some form of authority in regards to the area of influence they oversaw that directly affected parts of my life (i.e. pastors, teachers, bosses, etc.), they were not fathers or mothers to me. Why? Because they did not possess a greater vision over my life than I carried for myself, I could not give them a weighty voice in my life.

In contrast, there was a time in which I was about to make a life-altering decision by taking the lead role as overseer of a church we were a part of. I could feel in the Spirit that I was being called into a promotion, but I didn't know what it would specifically look like. I was wondering if that feeling of pending promotion was confirmation to accept this local church position even though I was not really excited about it. I was capable but not passionate about the idea. I ran the idea by a mentor and great friend of mine. What he said kept me from making the wrong decision. He told me, *"Bethany, you're not called to the local; your calling is international. And if you take the leadership of this local church, you will be setting back your life's purpose by at least five years."*

That prophetic insight did two things in me. It not only liberated me from potentially making a really bad decision, but it empowered me to believe that I was made for something greater than even I had dreamed of! As a result of that conversation, I did not pursue taking the overseer position of that local church and have since been traveling internationally doing what I was born for, and I have never felt so alive.

Brothers and Sisters

Brothers and sisters bring the much needed peer synergy to *"spur one another on to love and good deeds."*[36] These are the people you are running with. Brothers and sisters get to champion each other in challenging times, and they are the ones who Proverbs says are *"born for a time of adversity."*[37] They are going to stand with you and raise your arms up until the battle is won, just as Aaron and Hur did with Moses.[38]

As I shared earlier, when my youngest daughter was three, she became extremely sick with a severe case of pneumonia that hospitalized her for six weeks and brought her to the brink of death. When she was first diagnosed, my family and I walked alongside her through the health clinic where she was being wheeled on a gurney and into an ambulance. They were taking us to a nearby children's hospital so she could receive the needed care from pediatric experts. As we were walking out the door, my heart was heavy with fear and anxiety of the unknown. Lost in my concern, I soon heard guitar music and singing next to the ambulance. It was coming from a good friend who had driven hours to worship over Elli. My friend did far more than take the time to show up and express her love and concern; she was being a sister to me in that moment and was holding up my arms through worship until the coming battle would be won.

---

36   Hebrews 10:24
37   Proverbs 17:17
38   Exodus 17:12-14

Brothers and sisters are born for adversity. They stand by us as we press on through the dark nights of our soul reminding us that the light dawns again, and they stay with us until it does.

Brothers and sisters also celebrate our seasons of promotion without competition or jealousy. One of the things I have learned from Bill Johnson in this arena

> *Brothers and sisters are born for adversity. They stand by us as we press on through the dark nights of our soul reminding us that the light dawns again, and they stay with us until it does.*

is that when we celebrate someone else's promotion in an area that we need breakthrough in, we are prophesying to our own future breakthrough. God is the same yesterday, today, and forever, and what He did for one, He will do for another. So, I can celebrate what God is doing for you because He's coming for me too!

I love watching those I'm running with get promoted in areas of life they are called to. It is seriously one of my greatest joys to watch those I've run with for years be faithful in what they are called to and then a "suddenly" happens, and they are promoted into a new season of authority, grace, and power. It makes my heart so happy to come alongside and celebrate my brothers and sisters as promises and promotion manifest for them, especially the things I had prophetically "seen" years earlier.

But, if I'm honest, there were times in the past when I felt frustrated that I was still hidden or seemingly unseen. I remember one particular time when I had pastored and carried my local church through a particularly rough season. During those six months, I pastored, preached, led worship, organized other speakers and teams and even did the bookkeeping to keep my church alive. Though it was a very difficult season for me, God's grace was always present every step of the way. When the new pastor was set in, I was thrilled and excited because it was not my assignment to pastor this church long term. As the young pastor began to move forward in his promotion and build his new leadership team, though I and my husband seemed like a natural choice to be included in that team, we weren't chosen, and, honestly, it tweaked me for a short time.

As I was processing with the Lord about this, I heard Him ask me, *"Do you believe he is My choice to pastor the church?"* I said, "Yes, Lord! I totally know he is your choice!" He replied, *"Since you believe he is My choice, why do you care if you're not his choice?"*

Wow. That gave my heart a new perspective. As a result, I was able to release my own issues of offense that were attached to his promotion and celebrate that God had him exactly where he was supposed to be. This young pastor loved and valued me and my husband, but I wasn't supposed to be a part of his local leadership team. I believe he had heard the Lord on that!

Because I was able to celebrate him as a brother who is running in his promotion, I was able to step into my own upgrade a short time later when the Lord moved my family to a different city where I was fast-tracked and accelerated into the leadership team at our new local church, The

Mission. In hindsight, I wasn't supposed to be a part of the newly formed leadership team at my previous church because I wasn't building there anymore, and God was protecting both the new pastor and myself in that.

God has given each of us our own "lane" in which only we can run. Sometimes we run together parallel in our lanes for a season and other times our paths will part. When you realize and embrace the truth that no one can fulfill your call and purpose but you, you can let go of competition and jealousy and celebrate our brothers and sisters to fully be their awesome selves.

> *God has given each of us our own "lane" in which only we can run.*

Sons and Daughters

Lastly, we are all created to be conduits and to give out what has been given freely to us. I fully believe there is *always* someone we can pour into no matter how many days old you are in the Kingdom. If you're one day saved, you can give your testimony to encourage those who are just coming into His salvation. There is always someone who can benefit and receive from your encounters with the Lord.

Our sons and daughters are those whom we are carrying prophetic vision for within our spheres of influence and whom are connecting relationally with us as well. If people don't respond to your input in their life, than you are an outside voice and not a mother or father to them.

Know there is nothing wrong with that! Not everyone is going to be within your assignment or connected to you by heart. This is why we need various types and expressions of mothers and fathers. Each person is unique. What one person connects with and needs in a mother, another person would not allow or relate to in their life. The key is in finding those sons and daughters *you* personally connect with inside the areas of life God has given you authority in.

"You did not choose Me, but I chose you, and appointed you, that you should go and bear fruit, and that your fruit should remain..."

John 15:16

Each of us is called to bear fruit; it proves that we are connected to the vine.

Each of us is called to bear fruit; it proves that we are connected to the vine. Part of bearing fruit is sowing into the Kingdom relationships God has given you. As we intentionally embrace our family assignments, we will bear the fruit of maturing under mothers and fathers, celebrate the victories of our brothers and sisters, and champion our sons and daughters into becoming the world-changers they are.

Kingdom is family, and destiny is found in family.

Kingdom is family, and destiny is found in family. We are all a part of His Kingdom, and therefore, we are all family. Who's your tribe? Who are your people? Who is your "local" family in this season? Once identified, you will discover in them clues and keys to your destiny. We *all* have people we are supposed to be relating to as family right now. Don't wait for them to find you. Be an advancer and seek them out until you find those you are supposed to be connected with. My guess is they are not very far. They could be in your office, at the coffee shop, your school, your church, an online community, or your home. Whose well are you drinking from and who are you bringing water to? Identify the "who's" in your life, and you will find your dynamic family.

CHAPTER 11

WILL YOU MOTHER ME?

As men and women awaken to the need for the powerful benefits of mothering in their lives, understandably one of the first questions will be *"Who is (or will be) mothering me?"* It's important to distinguish within the assignment of motherhood that there is a difference between releasing the *mothering grace* and being someone's *mother*. Already, as I have shared this message in various places, people have come up to me asking for me to "mother" them, and I hear the heart of what they are requesting. When you become aware of how powerful of an assignment mothers carry, who wouldn't want a mother speaking into their life? But the reality is, we aren't called to mother everyone around us.

Many years ago, friends of mine had some concerns regarding a woman who was intentionally building a relationship with their young daughter. What started out innocently enough began to cause concern when it became evident this woman was attempting to place herself as a "spiritual mother" in this young girl's life though she didn't have permission for that level of access. The woman's own unmet emotional needs began to look like motive for her attempted captivation of the young girl's affection. Secondary ulterior motives began to surface as well. My friends recognized this red-flag relationship and adjusted their daughter's exposure to this woman. We must be wise in who we allow to speak into our lives as mothers and fathers.

I believe everyone should have a mother's voice speaking into their life, but that doesn't mean everyone you speak or pour into should automatically be considered your sons or daughters. In order to identify who fits within the context of this mothering dynamic, we must first understand the biblical concept of metrons. Kris Vallotton and Dan McCollam have been key in identifying what metrons are and how they relate to our gifts and calling. Much of what I have learned and lay out here in regards to this topic has come from their teachings.

Metrons and Kanon

There are two important words in the Bible that speak into the reality of spheres of influence. The first term *metron* is a Greek word found in several New Testament references. Metron is your *"measure of rule"* or *"sphere of influence."* When Paul was speaking to the believers in Corinth, he stated that there are many he does not have influence with but that the Corinthians actually *do* fall within his particular area of influence.

*"We, however, will not boast beyond measure, but within the limits (**metron**) of the sphere (**kanon**) which God appointed us—a sphere (**metron**) which especially includes you."*

II Corinthians 10:13
(NKJV, emphasis and parentheses added)

Essentially, each of us has our own measure of rule or sphere of influence that we are uniquely created to impact. Think of this as the areas of responsibility that uniquely belong to you. For example, some of my current metrons are my children and family, the worship ministry I oversee, and the prophetic schools I help advance and train in. In the past, I also managed a coffee shop, pastored a church, and was the overseer for a Christian school. All of these areas of responsibility were in my particular metron. Dan McCollam says, *"The keys to understanding our place of influence can be found in the places where our gifts operate with the most authority, favor, influence, and opportunity."*

Remember, what makes a woman a mother is children, so children automatically become a mother's sphere of influence in which she has not only the authority but the responsibility to impact. If we don't mother our children, then who will? Whose voice will speak into and activate the destinies of those who are supposed to be within your sphere of influence? If not you, then someone

If we don't mother our children, then who will?

else will pick up that assignment, and we already see the devastating effects of the world's influence stepping in as a "surrogate mother" to a generation with an orphan mindset.

Free to Choose

One of the things we teach in our prophetic trainings around the globe is that your gift works everywhere on everyone, but it works best somewhere on someone. For example, I have a grace and gift to encourage everyone, but I have noticed that I have unusual *favor* with those who are within my metron. The people within my spheres of influence (worship, family, prophetic, etc.) are drawn to me without my really seeking them out. The apostle Paul understood this principle; there are those who are within his influence and also those who are outside his circle of impact. It's the same with us. Not everyone we have contact or relationship with are supposed to be those we are mothering. However, that being said, there *are* particular people you are meant to affect and influence, and your unique mixture of gift, faith, and authority will have the greatest impact on those within your metron. Understanding who you're called to and who you're not called to will save you much frustration and awkwardness in the long run. We are called to love everyone, but we are not equipped to influence and mother everyone.

> *We are called to love everyone, but we are not equipped to influence and mother everyone.*

Years ago, a particular leader attempted to use their positional authority as a leader in my life to impose a greater role of influence with me than they naturally had. They used language like, "I am your spiritual authority," so that I would accept them as a spiritual mother/father. It felt very controlling and manipulative. True spiritual fathers and mothers will never demand that you see them as such in your life. They will not require you to respond to them as spiritual parents in a devious or manipulative manner. That approach defiles the very heart and purpose of spiritual parenting, and any abuse of this relationship can seriously deter the impact of other true mothers and fathers speaking into their life.

> *True spiritual fathers and mothers will never demand that you see them as such in your life.*

I also understand that this can be confusing when that authority figure in your life oftentimes holds some place of influence already, even if it's just positional. We can be conflicted because our desire is to honor them. However, for true mothering to be effective, there must be a *mutual* understanding of respect, honor, and even heart connection between the persons involved. Though many people today would radically benefit from having the input of a spiritual mother or father in their life, as mothers and even as humans, we must allow people to be powerful and make their own choices. Ultimately, everyone is free to choose who they allow to speak into their life. As a son or daughter, you may not always *like* what your mother or father says, but you should always feel that love is their highest priority for you. Their involvement in your life should always be for your greater good and the advancement of your destiny.

As a son or daughter, you may not always like *what your mother or father says, but you should always feel that love is their highest priority for you.*

Assignment and Relationship

We must know who we are assigned to influence so that we can reserve the full strength of our impact to reach *our* sons and daughters. Knowing who you are called to impact as you move forward in this assignment will allow you to put your best energy and time into the right people, thus producing the greatest fruit in your life and theirs. We can not allow ourselves to be distracted or deterred by the "little foxes in the vineyard."[39]

Jesus Himself had a specific group of people He was assigned to impact and around whom He aligned all of His choices. He was called to Israel and was laser-focused on that assignment. He would not let anything but *faith* pull Him away from who He was called to influence. Look at how He responded to a desperate situation of a woman pleading for deliverance for her demonized child. The issue for her was that she was not a Jew, and thus, she was

---

39   Song of Solomon 2:15

outside of His current assignment. *"He (Jesus) answered, "I was sent only to the lost sheep of Israel."*[40] That may seem like a callous answer, but Jesus understood He had a mandate to impact Israel first and foremost and that to go outside of His sphere of influence would take strength and energy that belonged to His primary call. Yet, He also has a high value for faith, and it was this woman's faith that pulled Jesus "out" of His current assignment where He could release the miracle she so desperately needed.

Even Paul the apostle understood the boundaries of his own assignment to the Gentiles.

> *"Even though I may not be an apostle to others, surely I am to you!"*
>
> *I Corinthians 9:2,*

and,

> *"We, however, will not boast beyond proper limits, but will confine our boasting to the field **God has assigned to us, a field that reaches even to you**."*
>
> *II Corinthians 10:13-16, (emphasis added)*

Both Jesus and Paul understood that there were limits to their impact. They understood that to be most effective in their assignment, they must adhere to those boundaries. We are all called to influence the world around us, and I love that not just one person can do it. Jesus needs His entire Body to own their piece of our assignment to impact the world.

---

40   Matthew 15:24

The powerful missionaries Heidi and Rolland Baker felt a call from the Lord in 1995 to bring the love of God to Mozambique, the poorest nation in the world at the time. They began their ministry by *"pouring out their lives among abandoned street children."*[41] Heidi heard a call to a specific geographic region in the world and gave her life to love the orphans, children, and people of that nation. Now she is affectionately known as "Mama Heidi" not only in Africa but throughout the world because of her great love for God's unseen children. As we have learned, the assignment of motherhood activates destiny in the children and lends strength so they can be who they are called to be. Mama Heidi has continually given of her strength by developing Bible schools, medical clinics, well drilling, church-based orphan care, and so much more to raise up a generation of sons and daughters who love God and know they are deeply loved by Him.[42]

Finding Your Who

Some of you are working with youth right now, whether in ministry, education, or even neighborhood programs. These youth are awaiting your mothering voice to activate destiny in their lives. Perhaps your favor is with a different generation of people. My own mother has a particular grace to connect with the elderly. When I was a child,

---

41   https://rollandheidibaker.org/

42   https://rollandheidibaker.org/

she would daily go to the local McDonalds in the mornings and have coffee with her "coffee club"—a group that consisted of people decades older than her. Her favor and grace to be received by them and her desire to spend those mornings with these people spoke of her particular influence with the elderly.

To help identify your "who" within a sphere of influence ask yourself a few questions: *"Who do I attract?"* or *"Who is drawn to me?"* *"What types of people am I really good with and easily connect to?"* The answer may be an indicator of those you are assigned to mother. Identifying the people who receive you best and your favor with them is a strong indicator of your sphere of influence.

> *Identifying the people who receive you best and your favor with them is a strong indicator of your sphere of influence.*

Obviously, young children living in your house are clearly within your sphere of influence. But, look around you even now. Are there people in your neighborhood who are particularly drawn to you? Do you have unusual favor within the community or city you live in? Pay attention to those places where you have unusual favor—the places that make you come alive—and look for those whom God is drawing to you.

One of the things I noticed early on with my prophetic gift is that I was uniquely drawn to worship leaders, musicians, and singers even before I knew they were involved or gifted for worship ministry. Often the encouraging words I would have for these people would come more easily to me from the Lord and contain more specific and detailed information than usual. I also observed how my favor with this group of people was easy and synergistic, especially when I needed to gather musicians outside of my local church for an event or conference. Every time I needed someone, I could pull from any regional musician I knew, and they would say yes to me. I never lacked having a full band. In fact, at times I had more people on the worship team than in the congregation when the worship service began! These worshipers were drawn to me, and I gathered them. I have been leading worship now for twenty years in various places and have continually seen an influx of musicians, singers, and leaders come to me. Whenever there is a shortage of musicians, I pray and call them in prophetically, and *every time* someone shows up to answer my call. My ability to easily draw and attract this particular group of people regardless of age or geographical location reveals that they are in my sphere of influence to impact. Currently, as the worship director at my home church, I am mothering an entire worship community and using my strength to help activate them towards their own destiny in worship and life.

As you learn to identify those within our spheres of influence, remember that your assignment of mothering works on everyone but it works *best* on someone. There are people who are looking for you right now to reach out and prophetically speak and activate the destiny that is in them. It's helpful to understand who you are called to and who is drawn to you so you can be strategic and most effective with your mothering grace.

It will not be necessary nor appropriate for you to announce who you are mothering—the fruits of your assignment will prove your position. Focus on loving and activating those who are called to you. Even now, I pray that the Lord will open your eyes and highlight those people in your life who are particularly drawn to you and what you carry so you can generously pour your mothering grace into them.

> *The fruits of your assignment will prove your position.*

CHAPTER 12

PARTNERING WITH FATHERS

A S WE HAVE DELVED INTO the beauty, authority, and power of the assignment of motherhood, the natural trajectory of this topic leads us to questions regarding the role of fathers. How do mothers *and* fathers work together specifically and practically in raising world-changers? How is the assignment of fatherhood uniquely different than motherhood? Understanding these dynamics is vital to advancing into our role as mothers.

We are not here to replace fathers. There is no way we could nor should we even try; fathers are uniquely created and equipped for their God-given role. Ideally, every son and daughter will have both mothers *and* fathers speaking into their lives so they can benefit from the whole picture of God's design and intent for Kingdom life and family. Obviously, it would

> *We are not here to replace fathers. There is no way we could nor should we even try; fathers are uniquely created and equipped for their God-given role.*

take another book to unpack all of the gifting, anointing, and assignment that a father brings to the family. Therefore, I will focus this chapter to only briefly touch on what I've observed, experienced, and seen in Scripture that a father uniquely carries.

Calling Out Identity

The first key to a father's assignment is his ability to *call* out the identity of who their sons and daughters are. This distinction of fathers to call out identity is first seen at the beginning of creation when God commissioned Adam to name all of the animals.

> *"He (God) brought them to the man to see what he would name them; and whatever the man called each living creature, that was its name."*
>
> *Genesis 2:19*

There is a God-given grace on men in particular to call out identity, and we see that most prominently in the fathering assignment.

A chapter later, we see that Adam named his wife Eve because he saw her destiny to become the mother of all the living; the name he gave her reflected her destiny. There is a God-given grace on men in particular to call out identity, and we see that most prominently in the fathering assignment.

142

In the Western world when a child is born, they commonly take on their father's last name. God has given men the responsibility of assigning identity to their children so they will know who they are, and it all began with Father God Himself.

> *"See what great love the Father has lavished on us, that we should be **called** children of God! And that is what we are!"*
>
> *I John 3:1, (emphasis added)*

It is God as Father who set the precedent for natural and spiritual fathers by showing them what to do. Just as God calls us His children, which is our primary identity, fathers are to call out heaven's identity over their children.

> *Just as God calls us His children, which is our primary identity, fathers are to call out heaven's identity over their children.*

As we discovered earlier in this book, a name carries identity, destiny, and legacy within it. So it stands to reason that when a father calls his children by name, he is proclaiming who they are. Their destiny and legacy is found within the father's name. My maiden name is Johnston, and though I am married with a new last name, I am still a Johnston in my DNA and spiritual inheritance. Years ago, our family researched our genealogy to discover what our family's name meant. In the process, we found a family crest associated with our name. The Latin motto upon the

143

crest read *"numquam non paratus"* which translated is *"never unprepared."* Part of my family's blessing and destiny is that we are called to be prepared for everything that comes our way, and if you know my family, that description is remarkably accurate. Honestly, the revelation of this family crest helped explain a lot about who I am as a person. Through it, I realized that part of my spiritual and natural legacy as a Johnston is to be one who is *ready in season and out*. Never unprepared. Always prepared to do good.

I have watched many friends of mine operate in the assignment of fatherhood brilliantly. One in particular, Dan McCollam, travels frequently as an itinerant preacher and prophetic trainer in addition to serving as one of the senior leaders at The Mission Church. Having traveled as part of his team and having observed him at his home church, I am constantly amazed at how impacted people are when they are with him. I'm amazed because though Dan is an incredible and generous man, I know lots of phenomenal people who don't seem to make quite the same impression on people's lives. He constantly receives emails and messages from people who tell him that *"that one hour"* he spent with them years ago changed their lives forever or that his brief input set them on a trajectory of destiny. How is he having that level of impact after literally spending only a few minutes to an hour with a person? I believe his impact is primarily due to the fact that he intently looks for the treasure of who heaven says each person is, and he calls them up to that reality. In essence, he is *fathering* them by calling out their identity, and because identity reveals destiny, his wisdom and counsel is propelling them into their future. Fathers call out the gold in their children. They assign identity by revealing to their children who God says they are. They give children their name.

Celebrating the Now

The second key to the fathering assignment is that fathers *celebrate* who their children are now, what they are presently doing, or their current accomplishments. This is a powerful piece that fathers in particular carry and is so needed. I don't know any child who doesn't want their daddy to watch them do something amazing whether it's climbing a tree, riding a bike, playing in a sport at their school, or making tough life decisions. Ingrained into children is a desire for their father's approval—for him to see and enjoy them where they are at, right here, right now. The beauty of this desire is that our Father in heaven has already approved us all through His Son Jesus Christ. We no longer have to seek His approval because we already have it.

> *"Accept one another, then, just as Christ accepted you, in order to bring praise to God."*
>
> *Romans 15:7*

Because we have already been approved by our heavenly Father, He has now established the pattern for fathers to celebrate and accept those whom they are influencing.

145

Interestingly, there are two places in the New Testament where fathers were exhorted to *"not exasperate"* their children because it would cause them to lose heart. The underlying thought in these passages is that certain fathers would intentionally provoke or stir up their children in a negative manner until the child would become angry or discouraged.[43] Why would fathers be singled out by the New Testament author and not mothers? I propose it is because these actions are contrary to the core assignment of fatherhood. Fathers are to celebrate not exasperate their children.

> *Fathers are to celebrate not exasperate their children.*

There are many ways that fathers can celebrate those they are called to influence. From my experience, I felt celebrated and approved by my own father when he took the time to really listen to me, come to my piano recitals or the football games that I was cheerleading for, or when he simply showed up to anything I was interested in. Knowing he was making the effort to be there just because it was important to me made me feel celebrated by him. Just showing up is a powerful way to celebrate your children.

> *Just showing up is a powerful way to celebrate your children.*

I had two spiritual fathers in my life spanning from the time I was a young child until well into adulthood. I

---

43 Ephesians 6:4; Colossians 3:21

think the bottom line with both of them is that I felt really seen and enjoyed by them. When I felt misunderstood for different reasons by others, both of these spiritual fathers "got me." They didn't just tolerate who I was; they enjoyed who God created me to be, and that gave me permission to not worry about what others thought. Since my "dad" liked me the way I was, it didn't matter that others didn't. His voice meant more than someone who didn't really know me. I was free to be me, and a large part of that was because these fathers celebrated who I was, rough edges and all.

Obviously fathers are not expected to celebrate poor choices or sinful behavior, but rather are called to embrace who their sons and daughters are at the core. We were created to be celebrated, not tolerated; fathers carry a key to this aspect of raising world-changers.

> *We were created to be celebrated, not tolerated; fathers carry a key to this aspect of raising world-changers.*

Championing the Not Yet

The third aspect of the fathering assignment I've witnessed is found in *championing.* While fathers are uniquely equipped to celebrate who their children are *now*, they are also called to champion who those children are *becoming* and what they are called to do. Celebrating relates to the present — the now. Championing relates to the

147

future—the not yet. One of my favorite verses in the Bible is found in the Book of Jeremiah where God tells us His ideas for our future.

> *"'For I know the plans I have for you,' declares the Lord, 'plans to prosper you and not to harm you, plans to give you hope and a future.'"*
>
> *Jeremiah 29:11*

> *Part of the fathering assignment is to champion those good plans and futures for your children until they are a reality.*

From the foundations of the earth, every person on the planet has good plans destined for them by the Father. Part of the fathering assignment is to champion those good plans and futures for your children until they are a reality. One of the primary definitions of the verb *champion* is to *"support the cause of; defend."* Fathers are called to support the cause of those they are influencing. They are to defend and promote God's ultimate plans for a prosperous future and hope for their sons and daughters.

I remember one day I walked into my spiritual father's office. Pastor Steve was the assistant pastor of the church I grew up in. At nineteen, I had had an encounter with the Lord and had rededicated a wholehearted commitment to Him. Though I was excited to explore the new possibilities of the Kingdom, I also now felt somewhat aimless. I couldn't do what I used to do anymore because I did not have an appetite for the world any longer, but I was also new to being 'all-in' in the Kingdom and didn't know how to navigate it yet. As I plopped down onto a chair in his office, I said something like this, *"I need to DO something! Is there anything I can be useful in that I would enjoy? What do you see in me that I can move forward and feel purpose in?"* Thankfully, Pastor Steve was not condescending and did not tell me I had to wait until I was more "spiritually mature" before I could be useful to the Kingdom. No, he was a good father, and he wisely gave me a job. He put me in charge of organizing various events for the church including a large family camp, a missions trip to Asia, and multiple fundraiser activities. All of these things at the time were exciting, fun, and even creative for me, and I enjoyed feeling purposeful for God. But more than that, I felt championed by my spiritual father who saw my potential and made the risky decision of putting a teenager in a responsible position. Years later, I am still using skills I learned during that time period but on a much larger scale as I now oversee and activate large teams of people.

My natural father has always championed me as well. Even though he may not have fully understood where I was headed in my life. Recently, my parents have chosen to sow financially into me and my sister because they believe in who we are called to be. They are supporting our futures by sowing prayerfully and financially into our lives as an offering to the Lord. The Bible reveals that,

"Where your treasure is, there your heart will be also."[44] My parents are revealing where their hearts are by where they are placing their earthly treasure. Their actions are saying, *"It is our delight to champion and support our children's destinies and futures."*

Synergy

Hopefully, you can see how some of the keys a father carries are distinctly different and yet complementary to what a mother brings to the family. While a father's prima-ry assignment is to call, celebrate, and champion, a mother's assignment is to affirm, assist, and accelerate. A mother affirms what a father calls out. A mother assists and accelerates what is celebrated and championed by the father. Fathers are the *identifiers*, and mothers are the *activators*. While a father says, *"You can do it!"*, a mother says, *"Let me show you how."* Though many of us have often not experienced the fullness of these mothering and fathering assignments in our lives, it can

> *While a father's primary assignment is to call, celebrate, and champion, a mother's assignment is to affirm, assist, and accelerate.*

> *While a father says, "You can do it!", a mother says, "Let me show you how."*

---

44   Matthew 6:21

change now. *We* can be the change the world is looking for. We can step into owning our assignments now for the next generation.

Reflecting over my life and my own journey with incredible spiritual fathers but no real spiritual mothers, I can see now what the effect of spiritual motherlessness had on me. Though I felt celebrated and championed by my fathers to do what was on my heart, often I would have to figure it out on my own. I did not have someone who could walk the steps with me to help accelerate my journey, and I believe a mother is uniquely called and equipped to do this. I don't know what my life would have looked like if I had had spiritual mothers to affirm, strengthen, and accelerate the vision for my life, but I honestly believe I would have arrived to the place I am now a lot quicker if they'd been present. Thankfully, the Lord is always good, and He knows how to restore and accelerate lost years. He is certainly doing that for me now. But, why let that happen again? As women owning our assignment, we cannot go back to ignorant thinking. Mothers are powerful in the lives of children, and they are powerfully necessary to raising up world-changers.

There is a well-known saying, *"My ceiling is your floor."* The idea is that my breakthroughs, my authority, my influences, along with all of the battles and victories I have won, are now available for you to build upon just because of our connection. Christ modeled this same principle for us. His resurrection is now our resurrection; we no longer have to live in an inferior state of sinfulness, guilt, and shame. He died, rose from the dead, ascended, and is now seated at the right hand of the Father. His ceiling is now our floor, so to speak, and it's a pretty high ceiling! We are launched into destiny from the finished work of Christ, and we get to offer the same benefit to our sons and daughters. As a spiritual or natural parent we declare to our children that they don't have to fight the same battles we did because we can teach them in a short time the keys to victory that took us a lifetime to gain. This is how acceleration happens in our Kingdom family relationships.

Mothers and fathers partnering together is more than one plus one which equals two. It is synergistic and catalytic. It is the application of *"five of you will chase a hundred, and a hundred of you will chase ten thousand."*[45] Every family benefits when mothers and fathers are functioning in their assignment. Now is the time for mothers to arise and take their place next to fathers in the family of God. It's a powerful call, but you were made for this because you are created to live powerfully. Step into it, own your assignment and let's change the world!

> *Every family benefits when mothers and fathers are functioning in their assignment.*

---

45   Leviticus 26:8

Own Your Assignment
and
Let's Change the World!

Made in the USA
Monee, IL
03 February 2023

27042032R00095